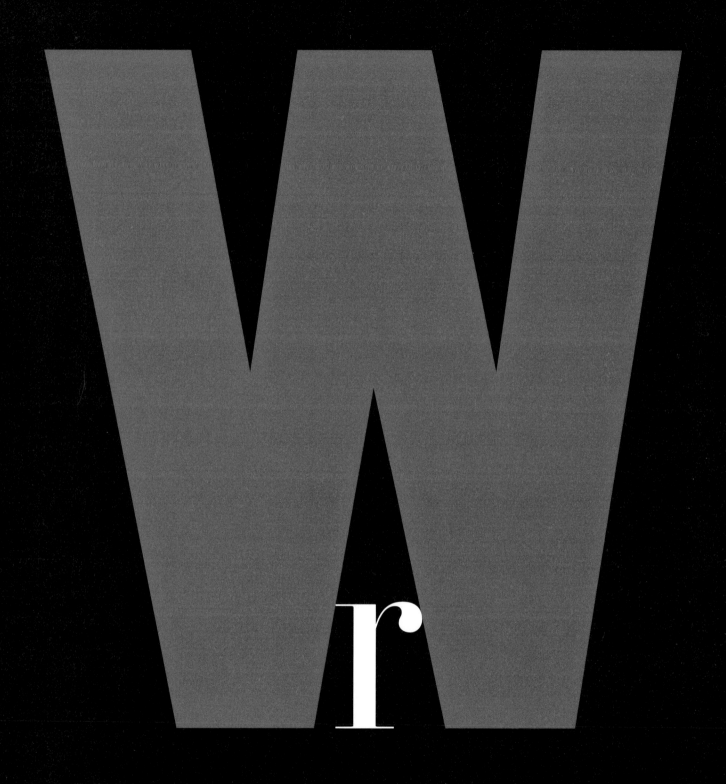

W r
WINONA RYDER

By THE EDITORS OF US   Designed by RICHARD BAKER   Introduction by DAVID WILD

LITTLE, BROWN AND COMPANY   BOSTON   NEW YORK   TORONTO   LONDON

A Rolling Stone Press Book

EDITOR Holly George-Warren
ASSOCIATE EDITOR Shawn Dahl
EDITORIAL ASSISTANT Ann Abel
EDITORIAL CONTRIBUTORS
Barbara O'Dair, Peter Travers, David Wild

DESIGNER Richard Baker
DESIGN CONSULTANT Fred Woodward
PHOTO EDITOR Fiona McDonagh
DESIGN ASSISTANTS Sha-Mayne Chan, Yoomi
Chong, Jennifer Chun, Robert Festino,
Amy Goldfarb, Anke Stohlmann, Bess Wong

First Edition

ISBN 0-316-89359-5

Library of Congress Catalog
Card Number 97-72966

10 9 8 7 6 5 4 3 2 1

RRD

Published simultaneously in Canada
by Little, Brown & Company (Canada) Limited

Printed in the United States of America

WINONA RYDER CAN MOVE FLUIDLY from playing a strait-laced wife in Nineteenth-Century high society to a college grad in Gen-X hell without missing a beat – only to trot back to Nineteenth-Century New England as a first-wave feminist. Then she can follow that up with her most provocative, and sexual, role yet: oddly enough, that of a Seventeenth-Century teenage vixen. This, from a young woman who made sure in the late Eighties that "Heathers" would enter the contemporary lexicon as a name for cliquey teenage queens – from outside the clique, that is. • Her success in period pieces of all types cannot be chalked up simply to knowing how to wear a bodice. It is because, as a selective actress willing to stretch, Winona Ryder, at twenty-five, transcends her time: She's thoroughly modern (ambitious yet arty, thoughtful, even self-preservationist) *and* royal old Hollywood (just check out her Oscar costumes). • She's got the classic integrity and radiant glamour that endear her to the grown-ups, while her newfangled honesty and hipster heritage appeal to kids, for whom credibility and authenticity are the ultimate attributes. Ryder's presence envelops more than any particular project she's involved in; her reputation springs from her seemingly unstudied star quality rather than from any specific role. • For all of her cool pedigree and attraction to the edge (her only long-term boyfriends, after all, have been teen-angel-turned-wild-one Johnny Depp and heartland grunge rocker Dave Pirner), Ryder's a composite of characteristics from the archival American cinema: a dollop of Chaplin's baggy imp, a dash of big-eyed Lillian Gish, all girlish frocks and tremulous fragility. Don't mistake her, however, for timid: While her earnest enunciation pleads for you to listen and understand, the firm set of her jaw signals that you must. • *US* magazine celebrates the talents who continue to thrill, as well as those bright spots glimmering with possibility on the horizon. In the way that Winona is often two things at once, she seems to fulfill both of these categories. *US*'s editorial mission: to get closer. With *Winona Ryder,* we hone in on an enduring young star who consummately signifies the spirit of the magazine.

THOUGH SHE BE BUT LITTLE, SHE IS FIERCE

{ **WILLIAM SHAKESPEARE,** *A Midsummer-Night's Dream* }

I
KNOW
YOU
RYDER

{ *Introduction by* DAVID WILD }

OKAY, PERHAPS I DON'T KNOW WINONA RYDER quite as well as I might like to think I do. From a philosophical point of view, can we ever really know another person or – more to the point – an actress? Still, in terms of Total Accrued Winona Access, my so-called life has been far fuller than most. In exchange for the myriad of benefits that come along with contemporary celebrity, Winona Ryder – the single most talented actress of her generation, in my not-so-humble opinion – has on numerous occasions had to waste a considerable amount of her valuable time with me – a pitiful bit player whose last dramatic performance was in a particularly hellish prep-school production of Sartre's *No Exit.*

We first met back in 1991 for the purpose of doing a *Rolling Stone* cover story. She had most recently appeared in *Edward Scissorhands,* so this was during what future historians might someday tag as the second of what will almost certainly be many waves of Winonamania. Ryder immediately and forever endeared herself to me when she explained, "Most interviews of actresses that I read make me want to throw up."

My hopefully nonvomitous story was for one of the magazine's annual "Hot" issues, and the headline of the piece read "Winona Ryder Beats the Heat" – that's a feat that this little movie star continues to accomplish with truly amazing grace. Never much of a slacker herself, despite being an icon of sorts

for that now endangered species, Ryder had already been named "Hot Actress" by the magazine once before in 1989, the year of both her breakthrough film *Heathers* and – lest we forget her profound precociousness – her eighteenth birthday.

DURING ONE OF OUR TIMES TOGETHER – amid record shopping, restaurant hopping and her helpful hints on how to avoid parking tickets in Los Angeles – it came to pass that I'd somehow managed to lose one of our main interview tapes. Such are the potential dangers involved in this sort of hard-boiled celebrity journalism. Eventually we would discover that the tape in question had actually fallen in between the cracks of a lumpy beanbag chair downstairs in the L.A. home where she and then-boyfriend Johnny Depp were cohabiting. But before we recovered the aforementioned tape, Ryder – an unusually generous and gracious sort off-camera as well as on – tried to save my pop journalistic ass by volunteering to do an instant replay of everything she had just finished saying. Being such an extraordinary actress, she actually convinced even me that I was hearing all of her answers for the very first time.

Ryder was – and no doubt remains – a charming and utterly disarming interview subject. When asked if as an actress she had any specific method – usually the sort of semipretentious query that self-involved thespians will gleefully ramble

on about endlessly – she immediately responded, "As an actress, I hate to hear actresses talking about their craft." I can still recall the lovably bewildered look on her face when I asked her how she felt about being a sex symbol. "I don't think it's the right phrase when you're talking about me," she said with convincing sincerity.

When I explained to her how many men in their twenties and thirties I knew were completely envious of my having the opportunity to spend time with her, she seemed humbly shocked. "You're kidding," she said. I asked her, "You don't get a lot of that?" She responded, "No. A general lack of that, actually. I've never done anything deliberately sexy. I'm relatively shy about that stuff. At the same time, it's exciting. But I'm really grateful that I haven't *made* myself on the basis of being sexy. With a lot of actresses, *that's* them. *That's* what they are, that's what they're famous for. *That's* what they've sold themselves as. Maybe I've done a couple of bad movies, but I never exploited myself."

All of which – here's the rub – only makes Winona Ryder that much more sexy.

YEARS LATER IN 1993, we would meet up for another long interview session. This time it was an on-camera conversation – well, one of us was on camera – for a *Rolling Stone: The Year in Review* special broadcast on the Fox network. At the time, Ryder was graduating from teenage roles to more adult work, having recently filmed Martin Scorsese's adaptation of Edith Wharton's *The Age of Innocence,* for which she would receive a richly deserved Oscar nomination. "It was the first time I ever felt proud of myself as an actor," she said of the experience. "It was a big deal for me to actually not be completely cringing and to feel like I made sense on screen for the first time – like *that's* why I wanted to become an actress."

When I asked her what she made of her earlier work in retrospect, the biting reality hit me of just how curious an experience it must be to grow up in public. Time and time again we have had the privilege of seeing her become a woman before our very eyes – indeed I believe I've watched Ryder come of age and lose her virginity more often than any actress in all of filmdom. Of such meaningful moments, a certain sense of intimacy, however illusory, is born.

"To be honest, I have to say I really miss my roles as a teenager because I had some *amazing* roles," she said. "Kids come up to me and say things like 'You really affected me' or '*Heathers* really got me through high school.' Not only did it help *them* get through high school. It helped *me* get through high school." Certainly few have ever weathered the awkward ages onscreen more gracefully.

Most actors and actresses who get into the game early end up robbing convenience stores, or so it seems, but there are exceptions like Jodie Foster and Ryder. "I've been really lucky," she told the *San Francisco Examiner*'s Joan Smith in March 1994. "I can count on one hand the actors who have

survived going through adolescence on screen. But growing up in the Bay Area, I avoided the traps kids fell into in Hollywood. I've made a lot of movies, but I would make them during the summer. I stayed in public school. I didn't lead some kind of weird, sheltered movie-star life."

THERE HAVE BEEN OTHER HAPPY Ryder run-ins over the years. One time shortly after moving to Los Angeles, I found myself at Roxbury, a then très trendy club where – if I recall my tabloids correctly – Ryder's onetime *Heathers* colleague Shannen Doherty enjoyed some of her most headline-grabbing cat fighting. The event was a record release party held in honor of Cher, who played Ryder's mom in *Mermaids.* Sometime during that long Hollywood night, I vividly recall standing by a bar with Ryder and Cher's daughter, Chastity Bono, and hearing myself saying the following words: "I'm sorry, Chas, do you know Noni?" It was at that exact moment that I knew I was truly in L.A.

A few grungy years later, my wife and I ran into Ryder and her then-beau Dave Pirner of Soul Asylum backstage at McCabe's – a tiny Santa Monica club run in the back of a guitar shop – for a VIP-heavy show at which Pirner and Asylum band mate Dan Murphy, Beck and Liz Phair were all performing. Even with all the alternative heat in the house that night, Ryder – who has been an alternative hero in her own right since *Heathers* – still seemed like the coolest person in the crowd. That's only fitting: Years before Kurt Cobain captured the smell of a new teen spirit, Ryder's inspired readings of Daniel Waters's groundbreaking *Heathers* gave voice to the shock of a new X-rated generation. If that film's still-resonant lines like "My teen angst bullshit has a body count" or "I'm gonna have to send my SAT scores to San Quentin instead of Stanford" didn't make a vivid impression on you, too, then to paraphrase Heather Chambers, "Fuck yourself gently with a chain saw."

But enough cussing and name-dropping, especially since I keep dropping the same name over and over again. This Winona-dropping, if you will, may reinforce my worthiness to write this lovely book's introduction, but despite all appearances, that's not my point here. For when I say that I *know* Ryder, I mean *knowing* neither in the Hollywood nor the biblical senses. Rather, I speak not so much for myself but for the entire community of dedicated Winona watchers, those tasteful right-minded masses who for more than a decade now have sat happily in darkened movie theaters around the world feeling as though we know her. We are strong in numbers, certainly, but we are far stronger in our sense of connection with her, this gifted woman with what must be the biggest and most singularly expressive eyes on earth.

Why exactly do we feel this connection with Ryder? For those of us who were hit head-on by *Heathers,* why will we always see her as the queen of Westerburg High in our minds? Though only five foot four and about a hundred pounds, she looms large in our minds and hearts. She stands

I LOVE ACTING! ACTING CAN BRING PEOPLE JOY, JUST LIKE READING A BOOK CAN BRING PEOPLE JOY.

I LOVE DOING OTHER THINGS BESIDES ACTING. I LIKE MY LIFE, I LIKE WHAT I DO AND IT'S OKAY.

far apart from so many of her contemporaries – to the point where it seems as though they are barely in the same business. Consider for a moment that Winona Ryder is the Queen of Young Hollywood without really seeming to be a part of it. That's because in a sense, she's *not*. Sure, she's occasionally spotted at a cool club and sometimes she dates someone else prominent or even hangs out at a party with Courtney Love. Yes, former beau Johnny Depp did bankroll that Viper Room, our postpunk Algonquin. But virtually alone among actors her age, Winona Ryder actually seems to be focused not on the movable feast of fame but on her work as an actress.

T O HER CREDIT, Ryder also avoided being in any of the Brat Packish John Hughes movies that were all the rage when she was starting out in those carefree Eighties. She skipped *The Breakfast Club* and stayed safely away from *St. Elmo's Fire.* She was a nonbrat in her own pack of one. In 1991, I asked her about this. "Yeah, well, I'm glad of that," she said. "That wasn't ever even an *option* for me. And I don't think [Hughes] would have ever liked me, anyway. Those kinds of films are so corny. I couldn't believe how teenagers didn't mind getting those labels slapped on their back. God, talk about patronizing. Plus, you watch those movies and everyone is, like, thirty playing eighteen. It's just like, 'Get a life.'"

Winona Ryder clearly has got a life, of course, and more significantly, she's got her own way of bringing to life all the various characters she plays. To steal a phrase from our President, we feel her pain. And though, God knows, we should never trust actors or actresses *too* much, there is a fundamental, transcendent honesty and believability about Ryder's work. When we go Winona watching – an international pastime these days – we feel as though we are her, only with less luminous eyes, less porcelain skin and a less waifish but womanly figure. If she'd been born earlier, those hugely expressive brown eyes might have helped to make her a silent-movie queen. Those eyes have it. Even today they are something that her Northern California neighbors at Industrial Light and Magic could never recreate – she remains one of Hollywood's few real special effects.

Time for one more name-drop. Back in 1990, the talented but largely unknown singer/songwriter Matthew Sweet penned an exquisitely heartbreaking ballad of love and longing entitled "Winona" and in so doing tapped into a nearly universal longing in the hearts and loins of so many other Winona fans. Before the song eventually surfaced on Sweet's breakthrough 1991 album, *Girlfriend, Rolling Stone* writer Chris Mundy gave me a tape of the song, and I, in turn, gave a copy to Winona. Sweet was appreciative enough to thank Chris and me on the album. For me, that credit was unnecessary, because passing along the song was simply an act of solidarity between one Winonahead and another.

Frankly, I can relate to the song. Even those fortunate

enough not to be alone in the world – I'm a happily married thirty-five-year-old man with a child en route, for godsakes – can be excused for having felt a few stray pangs for Ryder and for finding her endlessly fetching. Her appeal is considerably different from that of so many other female stars. I think she brings the male of the species back to a time when we first came to see and comprehend the humanity of women. Her appeal is not so much that of the other, or the sex bomb, or the bimbo. No, she's more a seductive equal or, more accurately, a superior. Ryder is not the girl next door so much as she's the slightly peculiar – and unbelievably appealing – girl down the block. She's the Generation X icon, world-class thespian next door. She's the grand dame of the celluloid riot grrrls. Unsurprisingly, then, there are multiple Winona Web sites on the Internet. There's even a Bay Area band called the Wynona Riders. We like her, we *really* like her. Audiences love her. The camera loves her. And, in this case, they all exhibit extremely good taste.

U NLIKE MOST STARS of her generation, Ryder has led a career marked by an attempt to consistently make films that matter to her. She even appears to pick her films for – *get this, folks* – artistic reasons. Sure, we've spotted her in a few bad movies along the way, but we've never seen her be bad in any of them. Still, she is sane and in the crazed business of show and, thus, she has nothing against success per se. Her definition of success, however, appears to mean something more than just boffo box-office receipts. "I'm thrilled if one of my movies is a hit," she told me once. "But you should do what hits you. If I'm in a movie and I'm not really into it, then I feel like I'm . . . *lying* and, like, maybe other people will pick up on the fact that I'm lying."

Ryder hasn't believed Hollywood's big lies or perpetuated them. This is why the artistic impact of her quarter century on earth has been far greater than just the sum of her smashes. First and foremost, she is an actress, not a commodity. She may never be the box-office queen, and that may be part of the secret of her endurance. In a world of overnight successes and fifteen-minute reigns, she has been able to build a career over a long period of time, much like R.E.M. has in music, avoiding cinematic one-hit-wonderdom. "I became successful in such a gradual way," she told *USA Weekend* in 1995. "I was never in a huge hit that made me an overnight star. So I never got shoved down people's throats. I was doing movies – some were successful, some weren't, but the ones that weren't successful weren't 'a Winona Ryder movie.' "

Even if there is no such thing as a Winona Ryder movie, there may be an archetypal Winona Ryder heroine, a creature that was perhaps best described by *Time's* Richard Corliss in January 1995: "The true Ryder heroine is a gentle soul in tremulous transition to maturity. Not a fairy-tale princess, either, but a bright child, ripe for romance, who opens a storybook and eagerly falls into its pages – an Alice in search of Wonderland."

"Usually, you're a girl or you're a woman, and the in-between part was never really explored in that time," she told *Los Angeles Daily News* writer Bob Strauss while promoting *Little Women* in 1994. "It was just too awkward and disturbing for people." Ryder has spent a considerable part of her career exploring that "in-between part" with a seriousness and artistry that is worlds away from the commercial standard of the day.

If Winona Ryder is an exceptional talent – and she clearly is – then she also had the sort of exceptional upbringing to help explain it. She had what *Rolling Stone*'s David Handelman described back in 1989 as "an alternative childhood."

SHE WAS BORN WINONA LAURA HOROWITZ on October 29, 1971, near Winona, Minnesota, the town for which she was named. The Ryder part came much later after filming *Lucas,* when she was asked what name she wanted in the credits. Apparently she and her parents also considered Winona Huxley before finally settling on Winona Ryder. "I think my dad had a Mitch Ryder album on," she told me in 1991.

Ryder grew up around the San Francisco Bay area with parents who could fairly be described as more enlightened and trippy than the usual suburban Mom and Pop. Let's put it this way, folks: Her godfather was the late counterculture writer, psychologist and drug guru Timothy Leary, who told *Rolling Stone*'s Handelman, "I see Noni as one of the first members of a new generation. 'The Kids of the Summer of Love.'" Leary also described the Horowitzes as "hippie intellectuals and psychedelic scholars." (The pair maintained a relationship until the end: Ryder was with Leary when he died in 1996.)

Michael Horowitz is a dealer of rare books and magazines, as well as an archivist who runs a small publishing company called Flashback Books, which specializes in books about the Sixties and the Beat era. He was also an associate of Leary (for whom he served as archivist) as well as a friend to Allen Ginsberg and numerous other writers. Michael and Cynthia – who only formally married when Ryder was ten – collaborated to edit 1977's *Moksha: Aldous Huxley's Writings on Psychedelics and the Visionary Experience* as well as a 1982 anthology entitled *Shaman Woman, Mainline Lady: Women's Writings on the Drug Experience,* which intriguingly included a story by Lousia May Alcott, author of *Little Women.* In addition to Winona, Cynthia and Michael also collaborated on a younger brother Yuri, so named, in pre-glasnost spirit, after the Russian cosmonaut Yuri Gagarin. Winona also has a half-sister, Sunyata, and a half-brother, Jubal, both from her mother's first marriage.

When I met her, Ryder was tired of journalists tagging her folks as hippies. "My parents were not these crazy hippies," she told me. "Maybe my dad was part hippie, but he was more of an intellectual and an observer and a writer. Of course he experimented and did all that stuff that people did in the Sixties, but he was, like, on the intellectual side of things. He was doing it all because he was curious, and he recorded it."

FOR RYDER, ACTING BEGAN WITH family performances. At one point, her mom ran a sort of revival house in a barn helping to make Ryder perhaps the world's youngest fan of Greer Garson, Bette Davis, Anne Bancroft and Gena Rowlands. In her very first *US* appearance back in 1987, a fifteen-year-old Ryder told Leslie Van Buskirk – now the magazine's senior articles editor – how her mother passed on to her a deep love of cinema. "Ever since I was seven, she would keep me home from school if there was a good movie on," she said with a giggle. "One time, she made me stay home and watch *Little Women,* and she said I'd be grounded if I didn't! She gets really intense about old movies." Ryder's parents, in fact, once worked on a script about *Little Women* author Louisa May Alcott and her relationship with New York critic and short-story author Fitz Hugh Ludlow. Within the next decade, of course, there'd be a wonderful new film version of *Little Women* for young girls everywhere to watch with their mothers – this one starring Winona Ryder.

Some accounts would have it that Ryder grew up on a commune in California, but when we spoke, she begged to differ. "I never lived on a commune," she explained. "For a year, we lived in Mendocino in a house with a car, but it was on three hundred acres of land and there were other houses on the land–it was just tagged as a commune because people wanted to tag it as that. They wanted to make me out as a flower child. But it was an amazing way to grow up."

I choose to see Ryder not as some spacey flower child but rather as the best by-product to come out of that counterculture spirit of the late Sixties – with the possible exception of that whole stopping-the-war-in-Vietnam thing. While the rest of us were raised like veal calves, she was raised on cool. She joined Amnesty International when she was twelve. She went to Black Flag and Agent Orange concerts with her father. And perhaps unsurprisingly, her godfather Timothy Leary advised her to always challenge authority.

In 1981, the family moved to Petaluma, California, and as Ryder fondly recalled to *San Francisco Examiner* writer Joan Smith in 1994, "We grew up with an abundance of love and inspiration." As she told me a few years earlier, she benefited from parents whose thinking went beyond suggestions like "Just say no."

"My parents are like my best friends," she told me. "It wasn't like they didn't give me any rules. We had this relationship where I could talk to them about things that most kids can't talk to their parents about. I would say, 'What's acid like? Everybody is taking acid in my school. What does it do?' And they would say, 'Well, you know, this is the bad side of it.' They would take the mystery out of it. They would say, 'Well, you know, if you take it and you go to a concert, you are going to get a panic attack and freak out. If you get it on the streets, they make bad, synthetic stuff that is just going to, like, freak you out.' So I'd lose interest. Whereas I have a lot of friends who were just told, '*No,* you *can't* do that.' And *they're* the ones with problems now."

Of course, like all of us, Ryder has recalled a few moments of embarrassment with her folks, though hers may be of a more bohemian sort than most. As she told Lorrie Lynch of *USA Weekend* in 1995: "I was never really embarrassed by my parents, except by their hippieness sometimes. Like, we had this big bus, painted; it was named Veronica. They would drop me off at school in this, like, psychedelic bus, and that was awful." For me, she recalled a different moment with her father. "I remember one time he came to pick me up from school, and he was wearing a Sex Pistols T-shirt, and they wouldn't let him pick me up, or they didn't believe he was my dad or something."

Life being what it is, of course, not all was totally groovy and dreamy for young Noni. She has spoken a number of times of being beaten up by some misguided junior high classmates who mistook her to be a gay boy. Her school principal, she has said, somehow concluded she was a disruptive influence, and as a result she did home study for a period. Even this incident has a happy ending, as Ryder says it left more time for reading and that before long she started taking acting lessons for something to do—perhaps significantly the Horowitz family had no TV at home until Noni was thirteen.

Ryder eventually enrolled in a different Petaluma junior high. Meanwhile, she had found something to do, big time: She appeared as Auntie Em in a summer-workshop production of *The Wizard of Oz* and as Willie in Tennessee Williams's typically adult one-act play, *This Property Is Condemned,* at the prestigious American Conservatory Theater, where Annette Bening, among others, studied. Soon she was performing monologues from Salinger's *Franny & Zooey,* still a favorite work.

In *Little Women* when Jo March—the character she would eventually play on film—describes being drawn to write, we can almost imagine the young Winona feeling similarly about acting: "Late at night, my mind would come alive with voices and stories and friends as dear to me as any in the real world. I gave myself up to it—longing for transformation." From the start, Ryder had an uncanny knack for the transformation.

"We weren't thinking of her being professional," her mother told *Rolling Stone*'s Handelman in 1989. "We just wanted her to be happy, to be around more imaginative peers."

Ryder's big professional break came when talent scout Deborah Lucchesi spotted her nascent talent and submitted a screen test of Ryder for the film *Desert Bloom.* While she didn't get the role that in the end went to Annabeth Gish, it did get her an agent and eventually led to her getting cast in her first film.

THE ENTIRE INTRIGUING NONI OEUVRE begins auspiciously with David Seltzer's sweet 1986 high school film, *Lucas,* about a boy's life outside the "in" crowd. Throughout the small but deeply affecting film, Ryder turns up as the meek but adorable Rina, who clearly carries a torch for her fellow misfit. Not long after she delivers her very first

screen line—"Hello Lucas," for the record—we the audience develop a serious chaste crush of our own on her. Though we never get to know her as well as we might like, Rina is without a doubt the cutest, most irresistible ugly duckling in all of film history.

Among the movie's other accomplishments, *Lucas* proves that, yes, Virginia, there really was a time in Hollywood history when Corey Haim was a bigger name than Winona Ryder. The film, which also stars Kerri Green and an appealing, pre–Heidi Fleiss–era Charlie Sheen, is far more heartfelt than the usual teen-exploitation flick. And a short-haired Ryder brings her own unique resonance to every line she gets here, even "Wanna go to the movies tonight, Lucas?" and in the football finale, "Throw it to Lucas."

Next up for Ryder was the central role in director Daniel Petrie's *Square Dance.* In this earnest, stately down-home drama, Ryder finds herself acting opposite Jason Robards and Rob Lowe in a single film—now that is, ladies and gents, range. Ryder convincingly plays Gemma, a Bible-toting Texas teen coming of age under less-than-ideal circumstances, torn between her grouchy grandfather Homer Dillard (Robards), who lives in a small town called Twilight, and her troubled mother, Juanelle (Jane Alexander), who has moved to the big city of Fort Worth, where Gemma meets her older, mentally challenged love interest Rory (Lowe).

Square Dance is a well-acted and sincere piece of work, but it's definitely a rather slow dance. Prurient minds who appreciate Ryder's shapely figure—and we know you're out there—will perk up when her flamboyant mom Alexander tells her, "I know you told me it ain't happened yet, but you're gonna be a woman soon. You've already got the knockers." For the record, Ryder sounded an impressively dry note when asked about Lowe, then a major sex symbol, by *US* in 1987. "I guess I'm not the most up-to-date teen," she said. "I just never noticed Rob Lowe like all the other girls did."

WINONA RYDER'S NOT LIKE the other girls, thank God, and that fact is well-utilized by maverick director Tim Burton in his one-of-a-kind *Beetlejuice,* Ryder's first hit film. She makes a lasting impression on the public consciousness as Lydia, the sweet but morbid black-clad young lady who befriends the film's loving ghost couple (Geena Davis and Alec Baldwin), who haunt her shallow parents' new home. Michael Keaton's title character calls Lydia "Edgar Allan Poe's daughter" because of her vaguely Kabuki look, but that doesn't stop him from trying to make her his ghoulish, nonblushing bride. Looking like some brooding member of a postpunk Addams family, Ryder is supernaturally appealing as the tortured teen who relates better to ghosts than anyone of this earth. Even in this typically inventive Tim Burton gem, Ryder makes her mark.

If *Beetlejuice* was a trippy, freaky blast—and it definitely was—then Ryder's next film, *1969,* was a very bad trip indeed, a near-total bummer. Despite a talented cast that also

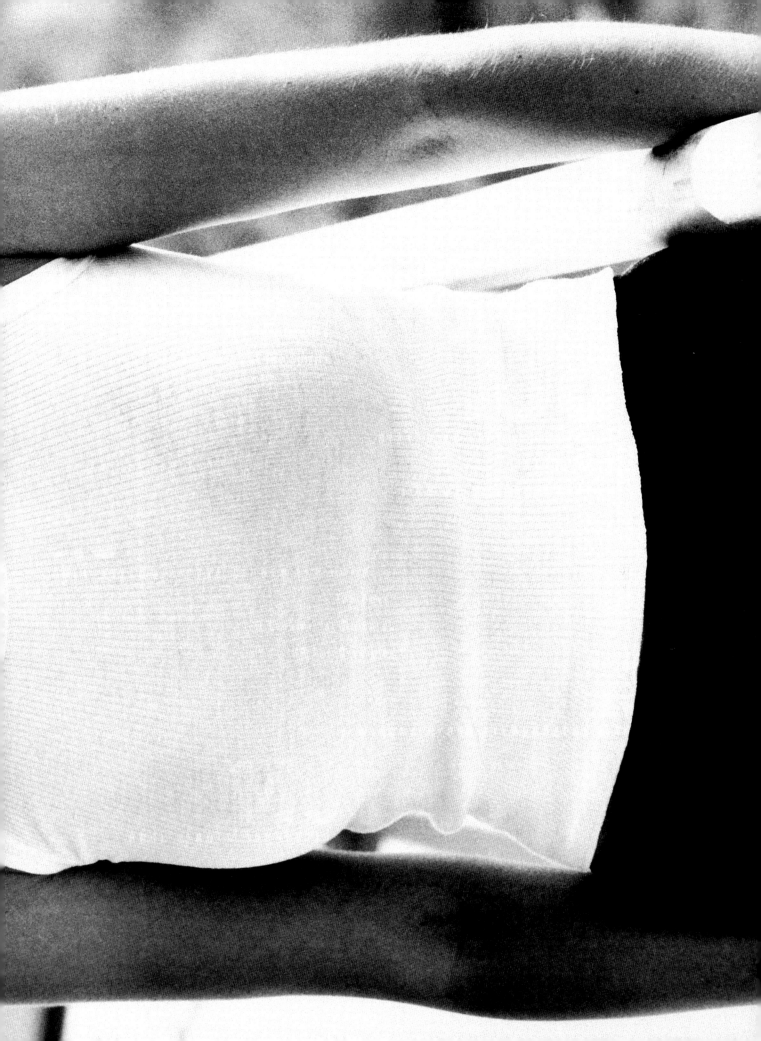

included Kiefer Sutherland, Robert Downey Jr., Bruce Dern, Mariette Hartley and Joanna Cassidy, director and writer Ernest Thompson (who penned the far superior *On Golden Pond*) manages to turn the traumas of the Vietnam War into a terribly hokey, tie-dyed soap opera.

It's a safe bet that we all could learn worlds more about what 1969 was really like from a brief chat with the Horowitzes than we could possibly glean from anything in this particular clichéfest. Unintentionally, no doubt, *1969* seems to last a year. Though hardly one of her strongest performances, Ryder acquits herself well as Beth, the brainy, war-protesting little sister of Ralph (Downey) who throws herself at Scott (Sutherland) with the memorable pickup line: "What am I, like, Rat Girl?" Soon after, Beth loses her virginity to Scott as the Zombies' haunting "Time of the Season" plays in the background. Typical of the movie's subtle-as-a-sledgehammer symbolism, this deflowering scene appears to unfold on the same night that Neil Armstrong walks on the moon. One giant step for mankind, one hot night for Scott and Beth. As a veteran of this misfiring war flick, Ryder was prepared for future cinematic squirmishes. On a positive note, the *1969* soundtrack was excellent. Shame about the movie.

THE SAME PROBLEM DOGS 1989's *Great Balls of Fire!* in which Ryder plays Myra Gale, the thirteen-year-old girl who became the child bride of her cousin, rock & roll pioneer Jerry Lee Lewis. The difference with this picture is that in the middle of director Jim McBride's mess of a musical biopic, Ryder, against all odds, gives a fantastically openhearted performance. At the time, *US*'s Chris Chase rightly wrote that she was "the best thing in the movie," and *Rolling Stone* critic Peter Travers praised her "vividly real" performance, which he deemed "smashing."

Indeed, Ryder's Myra leaves us breathless as she creates a giddyishly adorable young woman for whom it was well worth creating an international scandal, ending a career, and violating the Mann Act. Anyone falling for Ryder here is officially excused from the story's creepy, lecherous implications. But that's not the biggest problem with *Great Balls of Fire!* – that would be the Grand Canyon–sized gulf between Ryder's appealing performance and Dennis Quaid's wildly misguided *Dukes of Hazzard*–like impersonation of Jerry Lee Lewis. At times, his work in the film recalls Rob Lowe's performance in *Square Dance.* There's a whole lot of bad acting goin' on here, but rest assured, none of it is by Ryder.

In *Heathers,* her next film after *Great Balls of Fire!,* Ryder became a movie star once and for all. "I consider Veronica in *Heathers* to be *the* role of my life," she told me in 1991. In the brilliant Daniel Waters script – directed by Michael Lehmann – high school becomes what it has always been: a very funny and scary horror movie. What *Harold & Maude* was to the early Seventies, *Heathers* was to the early Nineties, a shocking state-of-the-disunion message, a cinematic wedgie

to those who thought they understood the American teenager. Ryder is the poisoned heart of the film as Veronica Sawyer, our window into the rarefied world of the Heathers, the school's female rulers who spout marvelously sick and acidic dialogue like "Bulimia . . . God, that's so '87." Ryder's Veronica is disgusted by the behavior of the hotshot Heathers. "Well, it's just like they're people I work with and our job is being popular and shit," she tells J.D., the new kid in town who's played by Christian Slater in his uncanny approximation of the young Jack Nicholson. Slater – who Ryder dated briefly – brings such charm to the role that it takes her awhile to realize she's in bed with a psychotic killer. "Noni was offered nine-thousand light-comedy, feel-good hits-of-the-summer movies," Robert Downey told *Rolling Stone*'s Handelman in 1989, "and she chose the one where she kills all her friends."

And though Ryder might puke at the mention of her bravery as an actress, she truly showed her guts in choosing the edgy black comedy of *Heathers.* Ryder has said that her agents at the time told her the film would ruin her career and that she would never work again. She changed agents. As she would tell *Time* in 1995, "I didn't do the strategic career-building thing where I make two big movies, then a small independent one, then another big one. I do the films I like." *Heathers* – with its unflinchingly wise-ass, cutting look at teen suicide and "Diet Cokeheads" – is a classic youth movie that remains a twisted masterpiece.

FROM SUCH HEIGHTS, *Welcome Home, Roxy Carmichael* – director Jim Abrahams's 1990 box-office disappointment – was quite a comedown. At least the film found Ryder back in black, this time looking even more like a pretty version of the Cure's Robert Smith than she did in *Beetlejuice.* Here she plays beautiful freak Dinky Bosetti, a small-town girl obsessed with Roxy Carmichael, the local hero who has left town and become famous on the West Coast. Dinky – an adopted oddball picked on by virtually all the citizens of Clyde, Ohio – becomes convinced that Roxy is her mother and that Roxy's ex-paramour, Denton Webb (Jeff Daniels), is her father. Her adopted folks, who are in the carpet business, make her feel like "a remnant." Abrahams – part of the *Naked Gun* team, that worked with film great O.J. Simpson – went on to direct *Hot Shots!* and *Hot Shots, Part Deux,* both starring Ryder's *Lucas* costar Charlie Sheen. Here, he has a few good insights into our collective obsession with celebrity, but even with Ryder's charming contribution, the sweet, slight fable doesn't quite gel. Like the movie's title character, the film never really arrives. And like our heroine, *Welcome Home, Roxy Carmichael* is pretty dinky.

RYDER IS WORKING WITH FAR MORE subtle material in the Richard Benjamin–directed *Mermaids,* an underappreciated 1990 film that was based on a novel by Patty Dann. Here, Ryder plays Charlotte Flax, a quirky Christ-loving Jewish girl growing up with a saucy single mom, memorably played by Cher. In a cast featuring fine performances by Bob Hoskins and Christina Ricci, Ryder is a standout as she demonstrates her unique way of playing both the ugly duckling and the swan, both of them beautifully. Ryder told me that she loved this role, and that love comes through in her delicate, affecting performance. As Peter Travers wrote in *Rolling Stone,* "the luminous Ryder again shows why she's one of the finest young actresses in movies."

Around this time, Ryder gave her most famous nonperformance in Francis Ford Coppola's *The Godfather, Part III.* Set to play the daughter of Michael Corleone (Al Pacino), Ryder encountered the first bad press of her life when she had to drop out at the last minute because of exhaustion. This resulted in many unsubstantiated rumors about the real reason she withdrew from the film and Coppola's casting his woefully unprepared daughter, Sofia, in that challenging role. A look at Ryder's film dance card demonstrates Ryder was indeed working at a fast and furious pace. A year after Coppola's disappointing sequel was released, she told me, "I'm really burnt out on even defending myself because the truth is so simple. I was sick physically and exhausted. *That's* what happened. It's amazing how people want things to be as complicated and nasty as possible. I think maybe some people were waiting for me to fuck up because I hadn't really fucked up yet."

S HE DIDN'T FUCK UP AT ALL in deciding to reteam with Tim Burton for the strangely moving, even magical fable *Edward Scissorhands,* a 1990 hit based on an idea the director had as a child. Here a blond Ryder allows Johnny Depp in the title role to steal the show and cut up all the scenery with a bravo lead performance. She plays a bit against type here as Kim, a popular girl whose family takes Edward into their home and hearts, who eventually comes to love him. There's great chemistry between Ryder and her screen parents (played by the great Dianne Wiest and Alan Arkin) and, of course, Depp. Ultimately, Ryder's is not the most interesting part in the film, although her characterization of Kim helps us understand instinctively why Edward might fall in love with her at first sight. Whether Edward's completely human or not, she's simply irresistible.

Though they were once engaged to be married, Ryder and Depp broke up in 1993. By then, she'd grown rightfully weary of discussing such matters too publicly. "I feel very protective of my personal life, especially my love life," she told me that same year. "I used to say I never read the tabloids, and I used to not read them, but I used to *see* them all the time. And I used to be bothered and say I wasn't bothered. And now I'm really not bothered. It's just hard when you're having a problem, and you have to read about it, and deny it." She broke into a laugh before adding, "Even though it's *true.*"

Perhaps Ryder's small but memorable performance in *Night on Earth* was her own artistic way of flipping the bird

to the absurdity of celebrity as well as a chance to work with the great independent director Jim Jarmusch (*Stranger Than Paradise, Down by Law*) and to act opposite one of her acting heroes, Gena Rowlands. In the globe-hopping anthology film, Ryder plays hard-cussing, chain-smoking Corky, the cutest wanna-be grease monkey ever to drive a cab. At the airport she picks up Victoria Snelling, a bigwig casting agent played by Rowlands. These two queens of quirk are incredibly entertaining together as their two very different characters develop a surprising bond. Eventually, Snelling decides she can make Corky a star, yet it turns out that she's perhaps the only person in Los Angeles who doesn't want to become a star. As she explains, "That's not a real life for me."

R YDER FINALLY GOT HER OPPORTUNITY to work with director Francis Ford Coppola in his feverish adaptation of *Bram Stoker's Dracula.* According to Jeff Giles's 1994 *Rolling Stone* cover story with Ryder, the experience was less than dreamy for her, as their methods clashed. Asked about reports that the director screamed at her, "You fucking whore!" as some sort of perverse stab at motivation, Ryder answered with her tongue firmly in her adorable cheek. "Oh, yeah, it was really great," she joked. "I love being called a bitch and a whore. It's a completely silly technique and it does not work." Ultimately, neither does this visually exquisite, big beautiful mess of a movie, despite hard work from a cast that includes Gary Oldman, Anthony Hopkins, Keanu Reeves, Richard E. Grant and Tom Waits, one of Ryder's favorite songwriters. The first in a series of period costume dramas in which Ryder would participate during the next few years, *Bram Stoker's Dracula* found her all dressed up with nowhere coherent to go.

Without a doubt, Ryder's next film – Martin Scorsese's elegant 1993 adaptation of Edith Wharton's *The Age of Innocence,* in which she costarred with Daniel Day-Lewis and Michelle Pfeiffer – was an entirely different and more satisfying experience for her. "It was a challenge every day to feel worthy of working with those people," she told me in 1993. "As much support as I got from everybody, especially Scorsese, it was like, 'What am I doing here?'"

Her portrayal of May Welland – for which she received an Academy Award nomination for Best Supporting Actress, and won a Golden Globe – made crystal clear what she was doing there. The performance, one of her most complex, was a great leap forward. As Peter Travers wrote in his *Rolling Stone* review of the film, "Ryder, at her loveliest, finds the guile in the girlish May."

Ryder repeatedly described Scorsese as the greatest director in the world, and he clearly enjoyed working with her. As the director told *Rolling Stone*'s Giles in 1994: "We had a very good time. Winona has a good sense of humor, and her energy is boundless. It was like having *rampant youth* on the set. She'd be jumping up and down, but then when you said, 'Action,' she froze into position. All that energy was put behind her eyes, and I found that really fascinating."

If everything went right with *The Age of Innocence,* then much of what can go wrong did on Ryder's next film, director Bille August's epic adaptation of Isabel Allende's acclaimed novel, *The House of the Spirits,* in which she costarred with an international powerhouse cast including Meryl Streep, Jeremy Irons, Glenn Close, Vanessa Redgrave and Antonio Banderas. Ryder looked lovely as usual – "The camera really does love her," Streep told *Time* – but the film itself was a multicultural muddle in which something obviously got lost in the translation. Here she gamely played a Chilean right-wing big shot's daughter who risks everything and falls in love with a revolutionary leader – hey, it's safer than dating actors and rock stars.

After all her recent drama and costumes, Ryder told Mark Morrison in *US* in 1994 that "I really wanted to wear jeans and lighten up a little bit." She did both to fine effect in *Reality Bites,* a sly romantic comedy directed by Ben Stiller. Some critics mistook the film for a feature-length Generation X infomercial. It had been a while since we'd witnessed Ryder acting with people her own age, and it was great to see her in *Reality Bites*'s "den of slack," surrounded by a cast including Stiller, Ethan Hawke and Janeane Garofalo. In particular, Ryder and Garofalo have great comic chemistry – someone sign them up for a series of buddy comedies *now.* As Lelaina Pierce, an aspiring documentary filmmaker who doesn't want to sell out, Ryder "can crack a joke one minute and crush your heart the next without breaking character or letting the acting show," wrote Peter Travers in his *Rolling Stone* review of the movie.

Memo to those on boyfriend alert: Take note of the cameo appearance in the film of Soul Asylum's singer/songwriter Dave Pirner, Ryder's then beau. In 1995, *Time*'s Richard Corliss would describe Ryder and Pirner as "more George and Gracie than Sid and Nancy." In Jeff Giles's *Rolling Stone* piece, Pirner also shared a loving insight into a quality about Ryder that is – for an actress – wonderfully unself-conscious. Pressed by the writer to explain her appeal as an actress, Ryder turned to Pirner and asked, "What's my appeal, Dave?" Pirner hit on something when he answered, "Your appeal is that you don't know what your appeal is."

S INCE WINONA RYDER grew up loving *Little Women,* it was not surprising that one day it would become a pet project. By 1994, Ryder's star power enabled Gillian Armstrong's film adaptation of the classic to get made – and made quite well at that. As headstrong young writer Jo March, Ryder gave a performance that earned her a richly deserved Best Actress Oscar nomination and – along with Claire Danes, Samantha Mathis, Trini Alvarado, Christian Bale, Susan Sarandon, Gabriel Byrne and Eric Stoltz – helped bring this timeless story alive for another generation. It was a pleasure to see Ryder working with such talented young actors as Danes and Mathis, for whom she had clearly broken ground.

About this time, Ryder, rather uncharacteristically, used her public platform to draw attention to a cause. Generally speaking, she ran in the other direction when actors started jumping on any political or social bandwagon. "My stomach turns when I see celebrities talking about things they obviously know nothing about," she told Jamie Portman in the *Calgary Herald* in December 1994. "It happens too much. I've spoken to these people – and, my God, they don't know what they're talking about! If they were interviewed by a real journalist, they'd do badly for their cause because they have no clue." But in October of 1993, twelve-year-old Polly Klaas, who grew up in Petaluma, was abducted from her home. Ryder was deeply moved by the Klaas family's plight and became deeply involved, working the phones, supporting the family and going public to put up $200,000 of her own money for information leading to the young girl's return. "I was devastated," Ryder told me, "and I was fortunate to be able to finance a reward for her. I had never been that close to tragedy before – kind of almost face to face with it when I was talking to the parents and the family." Klaas would be found murdered two months later. Ryder – who has a copy of *Little Women* that belonged to Polly Klaas – made sure this new film of Klaas's favorite book was dedicated to her memory.

In reviewing *Little Women,* *US* noted that the remake "could well prove as empowering for the training-bra set as the Power Rangers have been to the sandbox contingent." On the other hand, most of Ryder's costars in her next film, *How to Make an American Quilt* – Ellen Burstyn, Anne Bancroft, Maya Angelou, Kate Nelligan, Jean Simmons, Alfre Woodard and Lois Smith – were long past training bras and sandboxes. Ultimately their maturity only heightened the multigenerational vibe of sisterly support in the film, directed by Jocelyn Moorhouse *(Proof)* and based on Whitney Otto's novel.

In late 1994, Ryder told *US* reporter Trish Deitch Rohrer that she enjoyed working on the film with so many women. "There was the woman writer, the woman director and two female executives, and I was hanging out with all these really superpowerful women and thinking, 'This is how power should be depicted.'" Coming hot on the heels of *Little Women,* though, *How to Make an American Quilt* made it seem as if Ryder was intent on becoming the new queen of what some male critics have dubbed the art house "chick flick."

It remains unclear to whom Ryder's next released film, *Boys,* was supposed to appeal. Adapted from James Salter's short story "Twenty Minutes," the 1996 movie was directed by Stacy Cochran, who had shown considerable promise with 1992's *My New Gun.* Unfortunately, that promise was largely unrealized here despite a cast that also included Lukas Haas and, in his first significant film role, Skeet Ulrich *(Scream).* Ryder plays Patty Vare, the mystery woman whom Baker (Haas) takes into his prep-school dorm, then into his heart. Any film in which the male lead falls for Ryder has some core of believability. The seriously underbaked *Boys* has some nice moments but sadly never grows up to be much of anything.

PERHAPS, THEN, RYDER WAS SMART to turn toward a proven writer by appearing as Lady Anne in Al Pacino's long-in-the-works *Looking for Richard,* a lively and educational documentary in which Pacino attempts with great love and energy to brush up William Shakespeare for the late Twentieth Century. In completing that honorable mission, Pacino is joined by an impressive troupe that includes Alec Baldwin, Kevin Spacey and F. Murray Abraham to recreate scenes from the immortal Bard's *Richard III.* When I interviewed Pacino about the making of his film, he told me that "I thought it would need someone with Winona's essence and her sense of things and her intelligence, and also her openness and her vulnerability. And knowing that she didn't have that Shakespearean experience . . . her willingness to just do it, just give herself and just trust, was kind of inspiring to me." Me, too. In fact, I, for one, would like to have seen even more of Ryder's performance here – but perhaps I doth protest too much.

NEXT, RYDER CONTINUED on her literary beat, enlivening rather than destroying the classics by starring in Arthur Miller's *The Crucible,* as directed for the screen by Nicholas Hytner. Surrounded by a brilliant cast including Daniel Day-Lewis, Paul Scofield, Joan Allen and Bruce Davison, Ryder plays seventeen-year-old Abigail Williams, the vengeful young woman at the center of the 1692 Salem witch trials, which Miller originally used as a metaphor for the Red Scare of the McCarthy era. For perhaps the first time, Ryder played the antagonist here. And for a change, she found herself trying to look younger.

Though it had been her favorite play since she was a child, Ryder had assumed she'd missed her shot at the role of Abigail. "I kind of thought that I had lost my chance, with her being so young and all," Ryder told film critic Rod Lurie during a radio interview. "But I pretty much showed up in everything but pigtails for my meeting with Nick." The end result was a bewitchingly evil performance. As Peter Travers wrote in his *Rolling Stone* review, "Ryder offers a transfixing portrait of warped innocence." I even admit to being a tad jealous when Daniel Day-Lewis (in a powerful portrayal of John Proctor) screams out in court, "I have known her, sir. I have known her." Like him, I can only say, "God help me, I lusted."

These days, Winona Ryder is all grown up with somewhere to go. As she told *Vogue's* John Powers in 1996, "When I was younger, every time I'd open my mouth on the set, people would go, 'Isn't that cute? Winona has her little ideas. Isn't that *cute?'* Well, I'm not the youngest person on the set anymore."

Early in 1997, Ryder appeared on PBS's *Charlie Rose,* and it seemed clear how grown up she'd become. She came across as increasingly more comfortable with who she is and what she does. Ryder reflected on her days with Depp and spoke of how she related to the sort of attention that has more recently been focused on Brad Pitt and Gwyneth Paltrow. "All that attention is really hard when you're that young," she said. "I didn't know how to deal with it." As she recalled: "I didn't have an identity for a couple years there because I would see myself in magazines and think, 'That's what I am, I guess. I'm Winona. I'm this. I'm that. I'm precocious. I'm Johnny Depp's girlfriend.' I didn't know who I was." Time has allowed Ryder to look back to her first love with no anger. She told Rose the two are now friends and said of Depp, "He's not a bad boy, he's a good boy."

Ryder told Rose that there was no man in her life, though she explained that she and Dave Pirner were "soul mates, best friends." As she said, "I've only had two real boyfriends in my life, and I'm friends with both of them, so I'm very lucky." And in a time when interest in the personal lives of celebrities has become the national pastime, Ryder has reached the stage where her relationships become headline news – in 1996 just a few dates with *The X-Files* hunk David Duchovny turned into an overly explained media phenomenon.

Whoever turns out to be the fortunate bastard who becomes Ryder's betrothed, well, that's her business. But on a professional level, she's her own woman and seems to be taking more and more control of her own career, even optioning works that mean something to her, such as Susanna Kaysen's memoir *Girl, Interrupted.*

The last time I interviewed her, Ryder already seemed on the verge of such a personal breakthrough. "I felt like I was just this victim, and that everyone was staring at me," she said. "And yet, look, I'm, like, making movies, you know, what do I want? . . . I finally came to peace with that, and I finally came to this understanding that what I do for a living is a *really* great thing." Well, it is when *she* does it.

BY THE TIME YOU READ THIS, there will be a movie trailer hitting a multiplex near you announcing Ryder's costarring with Sigourney Weaver in the fourth film in the beloved *Alien* series, *Alien: Resurrection,* directed by Jean-Pierre Jeunet (*Delicatessen*). Come November 1997, get ready for Winona Ryder, pumped-up Action Star. Especially after observing her in so many elegant period pictures, it will almost certainly be one hell of a feminist blast to see an actor of Ryder's stature kicking a little futuristic ass just in time for the holidays.

A future with Winona Ryder – sounds promising, doesn't it? And because she makes interesting choices, it's hard to know what she'll do in years to come. For instance, can we perhaps look forward to *Heathers: Class Reunion?* The only thing that appears certain is that if she films them, we will come. So here's hoping that those famous words once tattooed on Johnny Depp's arm will ring true forevermore. Sure, celebrity relationships come and go. Tattoos fade. But true art – and true artists – are eternal. Let us do the right thing and tattoo those words on our collective consciousness. Say it loud and say it proud.

WINONA FOREVER.   **w**

HEART-BURN

COULD YOU BE MY
LITTLE MOVIE
STAR? COULD YOU
BE MY LONG
LOST GIRL?
T'S TRUE THAT I DON'T
{ *"Winona"* by Matthew Sweet from the album *Girlfriend* } REALLY KNOW
YOU BUT I'M ALONE
N THE WORLD

THE EDUCATION OF WINONA RYDER

{ By Leslie Van Buskirk }

So, Winona Ryder, what's Rob Lowe *really* like? "Okay, I've got this one down," says the fifteen-year-old of her *Square Dance* costar. "He was really a pleasure to work with," she declares, before giggling. "I guess I'm not the most up-to-date teen. I just never noticed Rob Lowe like all the other girls did." • Maybe that's because Winona (she played the lovesick lass in *Lucas*) isn't like all the other tenth-graders at California's Petaluma High School. While her classmates are off cheerleading or playing sports, she's doing a play or writing a screenplay. That's her mother's influence. "Ever since I was about seven, she would keep me home from school if there was a good movie on," Winona says, giggling again. "One time, she made me stay home and watch *Little Women,* and she said I'd be grounded if I didn't! She gets really intense about old movies."   ~ *US, April 20, 1987*

{ By David Edelstein }

MIXING BEETLEJUICE

Rolling Stone, *June 2, 1988*

It's hard to imagine someone being instantly in sync with Pee-wee Herman, but in 1984, when twenty-six-year-old Tim Burton was asked to direct his first feature, *Pee-wee's Big Adventure,* he brought something special to the party: a passion for wacko individualists. "I believed Pee-wee," Burton says, without a trace of irony. "So I thought, 'Let's just go through the movie and believe him, whatever he does.' I love extreme characters who totally believe themselves. That's why I had fun with Betelgeuse."

Betelgeuse, played by Michael Keaton, is the anarchic superspook of *Beetlejuice,* which Burton has directed like a cheerfully indulgent parent – he lets his little monsters run wild, to the exclusion of pace, point and structure. This isn't your standard, slick ghost comedy – the plot chases its own tail, and the jokes are a blend of the brainy and the infantile. The picture, a whatsit, has provoked its share of bewildered reviews. The fat guy and the other one didn't like it, and the *New York Times* said it was for people who think a shrunken head is funny.

Luckily for Burton, millions of people think a shrunken head is funny, especially when it sits on top of a full-sized body and stares out of bulging, doleful eyes. *Beetlejuice* grossed about $32 million in its first two weeks, and Burton has relaxed and made the most of his movie's addled reception.

"I've been enjoying the bad reviews," he says

ebulliently. "These bland newscasters, they have to say the word *Beetlejuice,* and they have to show a clip – and I don't care what anybody says, it makes me wanna see the movie. It's really funny. It's like you're watching some hallucination, like somebody's putting something else behind them that they don't know about. It was like the feeling I got when I saw Andy Warhol on *The Love Boat.*"

Burton, a former animator, thrives on weird juxtapositions – they're the key to his genius. His style is dork chic: He wears shapeless oversize jackets, and his hair is shoulder length. Under heavy lids, he has sad, spacey eyes. He's the sort of guy who uses words like "nutty" without ironic emphasis, who pronounces something "great, great, great – like, so cool" and then, to illustrate a point, casually sketches a bizarre creature with a second head coming out of its mouth.

Amiable and unpretentious, he has a whiff of stoned melancholy about him, like someone who thinks too much and makes sense of too little. And that's where he nestles his movies, in that twilight zone between the humdrum and the flabbergasting. If the two things don't quite gel, so much the better – and funnier.

"The things that interest me the most are the things that potentially won't work," Burton says. "On *Beetlejuice,* I could tell every day what was gonna work and what wasn't. And that was very invigorating. Especially when you're doing something this extreme. A lot of people have ragged on the story of *Beetlejuice,* but when I read it, I thought, 'Wow! This is sort of interesting. It's very random. It doesn't follow what I would consider the Spielberg story structure.' I guess I have to watch it more, because I'm intrigued by things that are perverse. Like, I was intrigued that there was no story."

'Beetlejuice' is a haunted-house comedy turned inside out: Its heroes are a pair of attractive, lovable ghosts driven bats by ghoulish people. When they can't take any more, they call in the title character, a "bio-exorcist." As played by Michael Keaton, with frazzled hair, rotten teeth and fungoid cheeks, the scuzzy con man blasts the movie into slapstick heaven — he's a sleazeball wizard.

Until his entrance, the picture has been funny in spurts but something else, too: goggle-eyed, a little sad. At the start, a couple (Alec Baldwin and Geena Davis) are killed in a freak accident; as ghosts, they learn they must remain in their rustic New England home for 125 years. Into their afterlives come the new owners: a screechingly tasteless sculptor (Catherine O'Hara); her geeky husband (Jeffrey Jones); and their sweet but morbid daughter (Winona Ryder), who dresses like a witch to express her inner weirdness. The ghosts aren't malicious — they just hate seeing their cozy domicile turned into a SoHo house of horror. So they do things like sever their own heads — while the living, who can't see them, remain oblivious.

If you've ever felt out of place, you'll plug into the ghosts' awkwardness — and into Burton's dopey, matter-of-fact surrealism. Aside from Betelgeuse (the spelling has been simplified for the title), no one quite fits in. The afterlife isn't grand and Spielbergian but a mangy series of typing pools and waiting rooms, in which you have to take a number to see your caseworker. Next to you sit horribly mutilated people in the state they were in when they bit the big one, but used to it now, so they're blasé, as if they weren't charred or squashed.

When Burton first read Michael McDowell's script, he thought he could have written it himself — it carried his trademark blend of the outlandish and the matter-of-fact. In *Pee-wee's Big Adventure,* for instance, the trucker Large Marge turns toward the camera and her eyes balloon out of her skull; then they retract and she goes on talking, as if nothing unusual had happened. And in *Beetlejuice,* Keaton's head spontaneously gyrates on its shoulders; when it stops, he asks, slightly peeved, "Don't ya hate it when that happens?"

The deadpan style resembles the great Warner Bros. cartoons, and the best gags are like jack-in-the-boxes — they zoom out of the screen and then snap back in. The disorientation is exhilarating. In *Beetlejuice,* Burton deftly blurs the line between a large model of the New England town (in which Betelgeuse, bug size, makes his home), "real life" and the afterlife. Bo Welch, who designed the sets, describes it as "a hierarchy of reality that leads you into unreality. Tim would encourage me to push that border. I'd go a certain distance,

and he'd say, " 'Let's go further,' and I'd go, 'Arrghhh!' and then be thrilled when we did it."

Burton lets his actors push that border, too. Catherine O'Hara at last has the sexy confidence she had on every episode of *SCTV* and considers *Beetlejuice* the closest she has come to her *SCTV* experience. Under bright-red hair, her blue eyes give her an otherworldly derangement; in a celebrated set piece she rises at a stuffy dinner party and – against her will – leads her guests in a spastic dance to the banana-boat song "Day-O." "The idea was, we were possessed by Harry Belafonte's recording," says O'Hara, giggling. "We tried to get that our bodies were really into it but that *we* were trying to get out."

The scene is a prime example of Burton's Inconstant: It's as if the little incongruities formed a chain reaction and mushroomed – a comic atom bomb. "The first time I saw an audience react to it, I got, like, frightened," says Burton. "I got chills, I was really terrified. I don't know why. I guess it's the power."

"I think Tim must be very secure," says O'Hara. "He knows what he wants, but he's also open to ideas." Take, for instance, Burton's collaboration with Michael Keaton. Keaton last had this gonzo edge as the enterprising morgue attendant in Ron Howard's *Night Shift* (1982) but settled down into more mundane roles. His last four movies have been disappointments, and he wasn't up for another.

"I turned down the role because I didn't quite get it, and I wasn't looking to work," says Keaton. In the original script, Betelgeuse was underwritten, vaguely Middle Eastern and more evil. But Burton wanted to change the tone and invited Keaton to come up with his own schtick. "I went home and thought, 'Okay, if I would do this role, how would I do it?' " Keaton says. "You clearly don't create him from the inside out. Meaning, what motivates this guy – his childhood or whatever. You work from the outside in."

Keaton really gets going when he talks about Betelgeuse, the way he must have when he wandered around his house for hours, trying out bits. "It turns out the character creates his own reality," he says. "I gave myself some sort of voice, some sort of look based on the words. Then I started thinkin' about my hair: I wanted my hair to stand out like I was wired and plugged in, and once I started gettin' that, I actually made myself laugh. And I thought, 'Well, this is a good sign, this is kind of funny.' Then I got the attitude. And once I got the basic attitude, it really started to roll."

And what was the attitude?

"It's multi-attitudinal. The attitude is 'You write your own reality, you write your own ticket. There are no bars, I can do anything I want and under any rationality I want. . . .' "

He stops himself from analyzing it too much. "At some point," he says, "you show up on the set and just go *fuckin'* *nuts.* It was *rave* acting. You rage for twelve or fourteen hours; then you go home tired and beat and exhausted. It was pretty damned cathartic. It was rave and *purge* acting."

"The thing I love about Michael is that he *gets into it,*" says Burton. "He'd say some funny thing that wasn't in the script, and we'd get ideas from that. I enjoyed working that way. My animation background – you sit around with a bunch of guys and talk about what would be a good idea to do. The whole cast was like that. It was this hallucination we were all involved in. We knew what we were doing, but we didn't know what we were doing."

"Credit to the cast," says Keaton. "Everybody said, *'We're in this.'* Everybody agreed to go along with this experiment. This picture is not without faults, but I'll tell ya, I feel very good about being part of a project that has broken some rules and is at the very least innovative, imaginative, creative – and just plain funny."

Like Keaton, defenders of *Beetlejuice* are the first to admit its flaws. But since when do great comedies have to be seamless? As its biggest champion, Pauline Kael wrote in *The New Yorker,* "The best of W.C. Fields was often half gummed up, and that doesn't seem to matter fifty-five years later. With crazy comedy, you settle for the spurts of inspiration, and *Beetlejuice* has them . . . enough . . . to make this spotty, dissonant movie a comedy classic."

The comedy classic has an unlikely hometown – Burbank, or "the pit of hell," as Burton calls it. "Probably his out-of-place-ness comes from growing up there," says Bo Welch. "It's in the middle of the movie business, but it's so mundane that it forces your imagination to work overtime." As a kid, Burton loved to draw, put on shows and play pranks – like the time he covered his brother in fake gore and pretended to hack him up with a knife. (A neighbor phoned the police; Burton still shivers when he talks about it.)

From college at Cal Arts he landed a plum job with Walt Disney Studios. "They were trying to train new animators," he says. "All the old guys had retired, so what was left in charge was these second-stringers. They were older; they were bitter that they weren't the ones that were in the limelight. So a lot of things besides creativity leaked in. What drove me nuts is, here you are at Disney – 'Best animation in the world,' they say. 'A dream come true.' And on the other hand, they say, 'Remove part of your brain and become a zombie factory worker.' The split that it created drove people nuts. So you either succumb or you leave.

"Classic example: I was at Disney, I was in animation for a year, I was totally freaked, I was so bored. They liked my designs, so they said, 'Why don't you do some for *The Black Cauldron?* Great, great, go wild.' So I spent months, I came up with everything under the sun. One thing I thought was really creepy: It had these birds and their heads would be like hands with eyes; instead of beaks there'd be these hands grabbing you.

"Finally, they brought in this other guy, Andreas, that you would consider classic Disney – cutesy little animals and stuff. And it was, 'Your stuff's a little, kinda out there, Tim, but we want to get you together with this guy – maybe the two of you can come up with, like, Disney but, like, a little different.' By the end of two weeks, we didn't get along – he was doing his thing and I was doing mine. He'd take my drawings and try to translate 'em. So finally the producer comes in and says, 'Tim, here's a graph.

This is Andreas and this is you. We wanna go somewhere right about here in terms of the style.'

"From that I moved into live action," Burton says. In 1984, Burton directed a live short story for Disney called *Frankenweenie,* the story of a boy who brings his hot dog back to life. The movie was meant to accompany *Pinocchio,* but the ratings board found it disturbing and slapped it with a PG rating; when Disney was shaken up in 1984, the film got lost in the shuffle.

Frustrated by Disney's inaction, Burton was liberated by a friend at Warners, who screened *Frankenweenie* for Pee-wee Herman and his producers. "It was the easiest job I ever got," says Burton of *Pee-wee's Big Adventure.* "I had a much more difficult time getting that busboy job six months earlier." In spite of horrible reviews, the daft little sleeper grossed $45 million domestically.

In August, Burton will begin shooting in London his most expensive picture: *Batman,* a $20 million action comedy that promises to go way beyond the comic books and TV show. In keeping with his taste for incongruity, Burton wants "to get a little more real with it" than you'd expect. "There's tension and insanity," he says. "We're trying to say this guy is obviously nuts, but in the most appealing way possible. I go back to what I thought comic books gave people. People love the idea that once they dress up, they can become somebody else. And here you have a human being in what I would consider the most absurd costume ever created.

"The villain is the Joker, the coolest of all. And also the flip side of Batman. Here you got a guy [Batman] who is rich, and something bad happened to him, and instead of getting therapy, he fights crime. But it's still kinda schizophrenic – it's something he questions in his own mind. And the Joker, something happened to him, too, but he'll do or say *anything,* which is another fantasy that all of us have – it's total freedom. So you've got two freaks. It's so great."

The split is pure Burton: One unhappy character dresses up to express something but still feels hopelessly out of place in the real world; another, an extremist, creates his or her own demented reality. Burton clearly identifies with the former, but the latter – Pee-wee, Betelgeuse, the Joker – clearly charges him up, inspires him to dazzling heights.

Both types have attempted to impose their personalities on a void – which is sort of how Burton grew up, as an awkward, artistic kid in Burbank. Maybe that's why he's drawn to any organic expression of character, no matter how clumsy. As a child he was moved by bad movies, the kind it's trendy to laugh at. "There's a lot of weird stuff in them – somebody had an *idea.* It went really wrong, and yet you can see somebody's strange mind. I love that."

Hollywood tends to quash such self-expression – it lives by formulas. But Burton slipped through the net, and he's hopping with joy. "If *Beetlejuice* turns out to be successful, I will be so happy," he says, "and so *perversely* happy. I'm for anything that subverts what the studio thinks you have to do." **W**

Great Balls of Fire!

Rolling Stone, *August 10, 1989*

WHEN DENNIS QUAID, duded out and blonded up as Jerry Lee Lewis, swaggers to the stage to pump a piano and sing "Whole Lotta Shakin' Going On," "Breathless," "Wild One," "Crazy Arms" or the incomparable title song, this movie can shake your nerves, rattle your brain and at the very least make you feel like dancing. Jerry Lee recorded new versions of his Fifties hits for Quaid to lip-sync (which Quaid does expertly), and the Killer has rarely thundered with more thrilling ferocity. Lewis's vintage rock is still cause for cheering. Too bad the movie that contains these Killer sounds never rises above a whimper.

Director Jim McBride and associate producer Jack Baran have adapted their lightweight screenplay from a substantially grittier 1982 book by Murray Silver and Myra Gale Brown. Myra, played by Winona Ryder *(Heathers),* is the second cousin Jerry Lee married when she was thirteen and he hadn't yet bothered to divorce his second wife. The movie begins in 1957, when Elvis discoverer Sam Phillips, superbly acted by the late Trey Wilson, set up the Killer as chief rival for the King's throne. The movie ends two years later, with Lewis a has-been at twenty-three, his career sandbagged by the media scandal over his marriage. His subsequent problems with women, brawls, booze and drugs, the hypocrisy of his preacher cousin, Jimmy Swaggart (Alec Baldwin), and the mysterious death of his fifth wife (he's currently on number six) do not figure here. Fair enough. But even an early film bio could and should provide insights into how a God-fearing kid from Ferriday, Louisiana, became one of the sexiest, scariest figures of rock legend.

Instead, McBride and Baran offer a candy-coated gloss on a combustible career. Quaid, whose recent work for McBride in *The Big Easy* showed a mesmerizing, maturing talent, is rarely permitted to cut deeper than a cunning nightclub impersonation. Quaid's take on the young, hotheaded Jerry Lee as a well-meaning bumpkin radiates scads of energy but scant conviction. Ironically, Ryder's vividly real performance as Myra works against him. Ryder, now seventeen, lets us

in on the confusion and conflicting emotions of this child bride without once playing down to the audience or patronizing the character; she is smashing.

To his credit, Quaid makes the sight of the Killer toying sexually with his underage cousin in a game of "creepy mouse," well, creepy. But the movie mostly dodges the Killer's dark side. We're told that lots of folks back home married young; that Jerry Lee really loved Myra; that maybe Myra wasn't really a virgin. Whenever the going gets tough, the movie gets going. After the Myra story broke, Lewis was reduced to playing dives. But the film ends with a full-scale production number. There's also a photo of a grinning Jerry Lee and Myra with their infant son, circa 1959, that suggests everyone lived happily ever after. Ha! Myra wrote of two people haunted by demons; McBride's movie plays like *Bye Bye Birdie.* Any which way you look at it, *Great Balls of Fire!* stacks up as something small, shriveled and inexplicably tame. Goodness gracious, indeed.   **~ Peter Travers**

US, *August 7, 1989*

BETTER TO LISTEN to legendary rocker Jerry Lee Lewis on records than sit through this version of his early life. The music is fine but the script just lies there, and Dennis Quaid, though talented and hardworking, gets into, but never under, Jerry's skin. The story deals with a boy who has huge, rambunctious talent, finds success in rock & roll and discovers too late that marrying a thirteen-year-old is enough to get himself ostracized. A good deal of the picture features townspeople bopping around to Jerry's music, and there are many (too many) scenes of him with his holier-than-thou cousin Jimmy Swaggart (Alec Baldwin). Jimmy tells Jerry to talk to God, "Just give me one hit record." Winona Ryder as child bride Myra, all big ears and eyes, is the best thing in the movie, followed closely by Peter Cook in a bit as a snooty English reporter.   **~ Chris Chase**

{ BY STEVE
POND
Rolling Stone
April 20, 1989 }

Heat

"I describe it as a movie about tee

hErS

"...angst bullshit that has a body count ..."

{ Winona Ryder }

No doubt about it: *Heathers* is a tough sell. Yeah, it's topical teenage comedy – but the comedy is black, and the topic is suicide and murder. True, it has a time-tested movie setting – a high school – but this is a school in which savagely materialistic students spend more time plotting to destroy one another than worrying about the prom. And yes, its lead is the rising young star Winona Ryder – but Ryder, who begins the movie as a popular but sensitive junior, turns borderline psychotic within the first forty-five minutes.

Heathers is a movie in which stylishly dressed high school girls smile sweetly as they say, "Fuck me gently with a chain saw," a movie in which a bout of bulimia is greeted with the put-down

"God, that's *so* '87," a movie in which nice girl Veronica (Ryder) falls under the spell of J.D. (Christian Slater), the pistol-packing new kid in town. Not long after that, the school's most popular kids (three of whom are named Heather, hence the title) begin dying one by one, and Veronica writes, "Dear Diary: My teen angst bullshit has a body count." It's hardly surprising that its screenplay was turned down by studios all over Hollywood and that New World Pictures head Bob Rehme — according to *Heathers* producer Denise Di Novi — has responded to congratulations on the film by saying, "I didn't want to make the movie, so I can't take any credit for it."

And if it wasn't easy to sell *Heathers* to Hollywood execu-

tives, selling it to the moviegoing public promises to be just as tricky. "They've brought me in on the ad campaign," says *Heathers* sceenwriter Dan Waters with a laugh. "And every week there's a new direction. It's like, 'This week we'll pretend it's *Fatal Attraction,* and next week we'll pretend it's *Beetlejuice.*'"

Waters, now twenty-six, began work on *Heathers* after he moved to Los Angeles three years ago. He'd never written a screenplay before. "I was working in a video store," he says, "and I was gonna write the greatest teen film, and Stanley Kubrick was gonna direct it." He drew on memories of his Indiana high school (where he was voted Most Unforgettable) but just as often on his younger sister and her friends.

He found his theme after becoming disgusted by the media's portrayal of teen suicide as noble. "You would see all these movies about teenagers wracked with all this pain," he says, "and then they would commit suicide, and their parents would be sad, all their friends would be sad. . . . That's not a deterrent. That's every person's ultimate fantasy – to see their own funeral." The screenplay Waters wrote was two hundred pages long – enough to make a three-and-a-half-hour movie – and far darker than the film that was eventually shot. In the original draft, Waters says, Veronica was almost like a "female Travis Bickle," blowing herself up at the end of the movie and then joining in "a prom in heaven, with all the dead characters coming back to life."

"It was really, really dense, very, very funny and very difficult to read," says *Heathers* director Michael Lehmann, thirty-one, who was given the script by friends he and Waters have in common. He had studied philosophy at Berkeley, Columbia and the University of Tübingen, in West Germany, before landing a job at Francis Ford Coppola's Zoetrope Studios. "It was overwritten in both the good sense and the bad sense," Lehmann says. "I don't know if anybody could have ever made that movie, but it was great."

Waters trimmed that script and softened it, and his agent sent the revision to virtually every major movie studio. "For about six months it was the hot script in town, the flavor-of-the-month script," says Di Novi, thirty-two. "There were fans all around town, usually among the younger executives," says Lehmann. "They all said, 'Well, we couldn't really *make* this movie.'"

Finally Waters's agent began shopping the script to smaller companies. Di Novi showed the New World brass Lehmann's USC student film *Beaver Gets a Boner*, which was designed to be a send-up of the typical heartwarming Lucas and Spielberg USC student film. New World okayed the thinned-down *Heathers* screenplay, a bare-bones $3 million budget and a first-time director. "When we got the green light," says Di Novi, "we were congratulated by every other studio. They wouldn't make it themselves, but they all said they were glad the movie was getting made."

On the set, Lehmann and Waters found they shared a sensibility. "One side of us is kind of pretentious," says Waters. "And the other side is always willing to undercut the seriousness of the thing for a good cheap laugh." They also kept trimming the screenplay, lightening the tone and eliminating things like the heavenly prom.

"We were worried," says Waters, "that if I said, 'I can't cut this,' the powers that be would suddenly stop and say, 'What is this movie we're making? Stop it!' We figured, if we can get 50 percent of the script on the screen, we'll have a very subversive movie."

Once *Heathers* was finished, Lehmann and Waters screened it for all the studios that had turned it down; they also took it to the U.S. Film Festival. It quickly became the most controversial Hollywood film since *The Last Temptation of Christ.* The folks at Disney, for example, who had loved the screenplay – though not enough to consider making it – didn't

like the movie. "The standard angry response," says Lehmann, "is that teenage suicide is not a fitting subject for comedy. Which is true to some degree, but we're not really making *fun* of teenage suicide. I think the movie does have a moral point of view, it does take a stance, it condones neither murder nor suicide, and it's so clearly in the realm of absurd comedy and irony and satire. . . ."

"The focus groups we had were really eye-opening," adds Waters. "You got to meet the people who liked *Cocktail,* people I never knew really existed. But there they are, and they *hated* our movie."

Now all they have to do is sell it to America. New World won't say how it plans to turn that trick (a spokesman says it's company policy not to comment on marketing campaigns ahead of time), but Di Novi says the executives at New World "to their credit, are trying to sell it for what it is. But to be honest, they've never had a movie like this. It's alien to them, and we've been struggling with it."

Dan Waters, though, has an idea. "I listen to Guns n' Roses," he says, "and I think that somehow we've got to market it with that kind of 'things are gonna be different now' subversiveness that they have. I wanted to do a trailer that said, 'You liked *The Breakfast Club,* you think *21 Jump Street* is a forum for hard-hitting issues. . . .' Then cut to the scene where J.D. says, 'Fuck you!' and gets his fingers shot off. 'Heathers, coming soon to a theater near you.' That'd get all of twelve people into the theater." He laughs. "Or maybe we should just misrepresent the film and make some money." **W**

{ REVIEWS }

HEATHERS

TEEN ANGST TURNS HILARIOUSLY murderous when Veronica (Winona Ryder) teams up with J.D. (Christian Slater) to rid their school of snobby cliques. Sick, but funny.
    ~ Chris Chase, US, May 15, 1989

THIS STARTLING SATIRE of high school sex and suicide deserved to be a smash for its inventive direction (Michael Lehmann), diabolically clever script (Daniel Waters) and performances by Winona Ryder and Christian Slater, who restore respect to teen actors after years of Brat Pack bungling.
    ~ Peter Travers, Rolling Stone, August 24, 1989

THE TEN BEST MOVIES OF 1989

[NO. 9] 'HEATHERS': Michael Lehmann's *Blue Velvet*y satire on teen suicide made for a seductive blend of fun and fright.
    ~ Peter Travers, Rolling Stone, January 11, 1990

HOT
ACTRESS

{ By David Handelman }

Rolling Stone, *May 18, 1989*

WINONA RYDER IS DOING something *totally* illegal. The sunny, dark-haired actress is blithely motoring around Los Angeles in her friend's rental car – and at age seventeen, she's too young to drive it. It's early March, only three weeks since Ryder moved out of her parents' house in Petaluma, California, and her own car is still up there, along with her collages, her bible – *The Catcher in the Rye* – her vast collections of handbags, socks, charm bracelets, Barbie dolls, *Twilight Zone* and Monty Python tapes. Oh, and the screenplay she wrote and sold. So just by driving to the mall, she's flirting with danger.

As Ryder reaches a major intersection, the traffic light turns yellow. "Should I go? No, better not." But she's already halfway across, so with one hand clutching her head in terror, she glides through, emitting yelps: "Huh! Oh! Uh!"

An oncoming car screeches and honks. "Sorry! I know, I'm sorry! That guy *hates* me now. Was that my fault?"

Her L.A. driving may be tentative, but otherwise Winona Ryder brims with self-confidence. "Insecure people," she says, wrinkling her nose, "don't fry my burger." Precocious enough to hold her own with adults, she radiates the qualities of a child who has always been encouraged: a chatty, optimistic disposition and an unself-conscious creativity.

"It's amazing," says her friend Robert Downey Jr. "She'll just call me up and say, 'I wrote another script,' like, 'I did another load of laundry.' To me, that's like bench-pressing the Sears Tower." While most kids her age are still months away from high school graduation, Ryder has already completed her home-study degree ("four point oh," she chirps) as well as six feature films.

From her first moments onscreen – in *Lucas,* filmed the summer after she was in the eighth grade and released in 1986 – Winona Ryder has been someone to watch. In her second film, *Square Dance* (1987), she had more scenes than costars Jason Robards, Jane Alexander and Rob Lowe; in last year's *Beetlejuice,* she played the character who kept her head while everyone else was losing theirs. Her alert, expressive eyes telegraph a startling combination of intelligence, gravity and self-possession.

Driving down Wilshire Boulevard, Ryder passes a gaggle of elementary schoolers in uniform. "I can't wait until I'm grown-up

WHAT'S SO FUNNY 'BOUT PEACE, LOVE AND UNDERSTANDING: AS BETH, '1969'

and have kids," she says, rubbing her tummy. "I want little boys. Want to hear the names I'm gonna name them? I like baseball names. Vida Blue Ryder. Cool Papa Ryder. Unless I marry some guy that has a better last name than me." She says she "worshiped" Dodgers second baseman Steve Sax for years, to the point of writing WINONA SAX on her school notebook. But the day he went to the Yankees, she says, "I burst into tears. The fucking *Yankees.* I would *never* do that, if I was a Dodger. It's morally reprehensible." (Besides, she had already "bettered" her own last name, Horowitz, when the titles were being put on *Lucas.)*

Though she doesn't envision getting married until she's *at least* twenty, Ryder is perched on the precipice of adulthood, rushed there somewhat by her recent roles. As Veronica Sawyer, the ambivalent high schooler in the daring black comedy *Heathers* – which Ryder made against the advice of her parents and agents – she deftly vacillates between a vulnerable teen scribbling away in her diary and an action heroine capable of murdering her best friends, all named Heather. And in the summer's *Great Balls of Fire!,* Ryder plays Myra, the child bride of Jerry Lee Lewis (played by Dennis Quaid); the movie includes a wedding night scene in which, as Ryder guilelessly puts it, "he's devirginizing me."

Ryder's incipient womanhood, however, is not without its headaches. Guys who previously viewed her as "jail bait," she says, are now making advances, and ill-informed gossip is driving her bonkers.

"I can't believe the rumors!" she says, rolling her eyes as she parks in the Beverly Center garage. "I'm going out with Dweezil Zappa. Alec Baldwin and I are getting *married.* Meg Ryan wants to kill me because Dennis Quaid and I are having an affair. And what's the other one? Oh, yeah, that the *1969* cast, Kiefer Sutherland and Robert Downey and I, are having a *ménage*-and-*trois* affair!" Her active eyebrows wiggle, and she laughs a loud ha-*ha!*

"The first time I heard things about myself," she says, "I was really hurt. People say, 'Just ignore it, or laugh it off.' It's hard, because *I* hear stuff about people and believe it. 'Ooh, really? She's a slut? Hoo!' So people are going to think it's true about me. And I'm sure I'm gonna be getting a lot more of it."

LOOKING VERY JUNIOR HIGH in a zippered sweat shirt, a white T-shirt and jeans (in contrast with the spandexed and moussed Beverly Hills mall vixens around her), Ryder rides up the escalators to Bullock's department store. "Stores like this totally scare me," she says. "They're so *colorful.*" She zips around making speedy but accurate household purchases – picture frames, towels – using crisp hundred-dollar bills, which she pulls from an envelope in her pocket. "I don't have any checks yet," she explains. "And I'm too young to have credit cards – which is probably a good thing." (She is also shopping for a house in the Hollywood Hills, which she says will be "very sitcomish.")

Out in the mall, Ryder whizzes by a drugstore, then backtracks and stares at its window display of shaving accessories. "Stuff like this really makes me want to be a boy," she says with a sigh. "It would be so cool to be able to shave. To be

able to say, 'Oh! I forgot to shave.' I used to sit and watch my dad shave. I think it's the coolest thing. I tried it, but then your hair starts growing back, like, *weird?* But I would never get the bogus George Michael thing happening. Like, perfect lines? It's so scary."

She pops into a store specializing in designer party dresses, looking for something to wear to the imminent Academy Awards ceremony, her first. A saleswoman in a billowy scarf and green leather pants tells her, "Because you're *very tiny,* you need something that's not cut too big, so it won't *dwarf* you." Ryder (who says she's five feet four "when I'm not slouching") grimaces and leaves, muttering, "I hate people like that."

A bookstore is next, where she picks up Kingsley Amis's *Lucky Jim* and Studs Terkel's *American Dreams: Lost and Found.* Then she pit-stops in a sporting-goods store, longingly eyeing a pair of sneakers that don't come in her size. "Mine are too stiff for basketball," she says. "My ankles flop all over the place. In high school, me and my best friend Heather [!] would get up in the middle of the night and raid my parents' liquor cabinet and go play basketball at the high school in the dark. It's so much fun – you don't know where the fucking ball's going! Sometimes we'd get up, watch *West Side Story,* then scale the school walls, get on top of the roof and do the Jets dances. We'd change around the letters on the scoreboard. We never had big word selection, but once we got it to say SLUT REEK when everybody showed up on Monday morning."

Throughout her mall trek, Ryder is never recognized by passers-by or salespeople. This blessed anonymity, however, is probably not going to last.

"People have been telling me that things might get a little weird," she says, heading back to the rental car. "People who know me know that I would have a difficult time handling fame, because I don't think I would take the precautions, because I have no sense of 'who I am.'

"The only time I ever feel like I'm in the business is when I go somewhere public and there are photographers saying my name; I get a really weird chill. I wish I could sit and think about it, but every time I do I get so nervous that I end up changing the subject. Sometimes I really sort of resent what I've gotten myself into."

DINKY NEEDS A BOOK BAG," Ryder says, picking up an old doctor's satchel and shifting it from hand to hand, considering its heft. She's at the massive Rose Bowl flea market in Pasadena, shopping for Dinky Bosetti, the obsessive outsider Ryder will play in her next movie, *Welcome Home, Roxy Carmichael,* which will be directed by *Airplane!*'s Jim Abrahams.

Ryder has been attached to the project for two years, and she's already accumulated cratefuls of Dinky's things – old *National Geographic*s, circus posters, etc. – none of which is mentioned in the script, and none of which is likely to appear onscreen. But this is part of Ryder's "method not done too mad," as *Beetlejuice* director Tim Burton puts it. The method began when she bought strange, Edward Gorey–like dolls for *Beetlejuice*'s deadpan, death-obsessed Lydia; it includes wearing an ID bracelet inscribed with her current character's name.

After scrutinizing the doctor's bag, she puts it back on the

vendor's table. "No," she says. "She needs a backpack. This is too uncomfortable to carry, and Dinky's a very practical girl."

As she wends her way around the aisles of bric-a-brac, she loses interest in Dinky and starts spending her C-notes on presents for her *Heathers* coworkers: a pocket watch for director Michael Lehmann, a silver belt for producer Denise Di Novi and antique fairy-tale books for writer Daniel Waters. She also buys herself a slew of hip, tasteful purchases: a silver bracelet with ceramic hearts painted with yellow roses, a sombrero pin festooned with sandal charms, a blue dress with polka dots, a black-and-white vest, a flowered quilt cover and a pillbox inscribed BERT (for which she concocts a wild history about a fat Mexican immigrant silversmith who changed his name from José).

She wears every purchase she can and lugs around the rest in plastic bags; she is shy about negotiating. "Before I started making money," she says, "I was a really good bargainer."

Farther along the aisle, she spies a trapezoidal bookcase, painted a zany aqua-and-black speckle. "This is very cool," she says. "Very Tim Burton."

It's true – the bookcase is right out of Burton's demented vision of *Beetlejuice* and *Pee-wee's Big Adventure;* so, in a sense, is Ryder herself. It's no accident that Burton and Lehmann, two of the best new young Hollywood directors, cast her as the voice of reason in the midst of cartoon chaos. She's hip and wacky enough to get the joke of modern life – and savvy enough to be able to play against it.

"Noni was offered nine thousand light-comedy, feel-good, hits-of-the-summer movies," says Robert Downey Jr., "and she chose one where she kills all her friends. She's a pure-at-heart person who knows that the darkness is all around her. She brings to light that there is truth and love even in the darkest impulses."

All this is probably news to Ryder. "I don't think she's into deep self-analysis," says her friend Lisanne Falk, who plays the least bratty of the three Heathers. "She doesn't think about it, she just does it."

"I think, I *think,* that I'm a pretty natural actress," Ryder says. "I try to do things as naturally as possible. I hate rehearsing, because I always like to save everything for when I do it. I just try as much as I can to really be 'in the moment.' I know that sounds corny and everything."

Still cruising the flea market, Ryder mentions that she's planning on getting QUE SERÁ, SERÁ tattooed on her arm. "I almost got it once, then they asked me my age. It's the greatest saying ever. 'Whatever will be, will be.' I was also going to get one that said BUDDY HOLLY on my ankle. Then again, I don't know if I'm going to get a tattoo."

The song "Que Será, Será" is used in *Heathers,* and the movie has clearly left its mark on Ryder's personality and lingo. She read the zingy script – "one of the best pieces of literature that I've ever read; it was the closest I've been to anything since *The Catcher in the Rye,* and that book really changed my life" – and latched onto it like a barnacle. During filming, she applied herself as never before. "I matured a lot," she says. "Before, I'd sometimes try to see how lazy I could get. All my directors had been more or less father figures, and all I'd have to do was be really cute and I could get away with anything. But it didn't work with Michael."

Not to say that she doesn't still have her ways. "She's got me totally bamboozled," *Great Balls of Fire!* director Jim McBride says affectionately. "She's just a kid, but she's been around the pool a couple of times, as we say out here. She's certainly not anywhere near as innocent as she seems. She was real nervous about the love scene for several days before shooting and indicated to me that she was very inexperienced in this area, and I had to sort of fill her in on things – verbally, that is. I took it all very gently and gingerly and tried to lead her there, but when we got to doing the scene, she leapt in with both feet and gave a very convincing performance. I'm not saying she's sexually experienced, I'm saying she's a good actress!"

The first time Ryder watched the finished scene, she says, "I got really embarrassed. I realized it was going to be in the movie, that it wasn't just what happened one day on the set. No part of my body is exposed, it's just that the camera is on my face a lot, especially during the pain part. And then she starts to enjoy it, and that was the really embarrassing part. The face I chose is really revealing – I couldn't believe it was *me.* It looks really weird to me: Dennis is so big, and I'm so little, I don't look a day over thirteen, except when I take off my shirt and I have this Fifties bullet bra on. I was just going by what I thought it would feel like. I watch these other people's love scenes, everybody's *so* sexy, everyone tries to be really subtle. With me, it's very different. I don't think I was very sexy."

WINONA RYDER IS COOKING PANCAKES. It's a bright Sunday morning, and she's bopping around to a Buddy Holly CD in the kitchen of the cheerful, desert-toned two-bedroom apartment she shares with a twenty-six-year-old aspiring actress named Kris Greenberg. Her bobbed brunette hair is up in a clip, and she's wearing a red-and-white gingham jumper, a white T-shirt and stockings and red suede cowboy boots.

"We need something more inspiring," she declares, replacing Holly with AC/DC's "Hells Bells." But after a few chords she decides that's not right either and switches to the light-pop group Fairground Attraction, singing along: "It's got to be-e-e-e-e per-fect!" "I like their songs," she says. "They're romantic but not depressing." But she prefers Fifties music. "It leaves more to my imagination, because I don't see the groups everywhere, plastered everywhere." Still, she does watch MTV with a passion, using videos as a sort of horoscope: "Okay," she'll say, "the next one is going to be a message to me about guys." If it turns out to be a poser group like Warrant, she gets depressed.

Pancakes are the full extent of Ryder's culinary abilities, but she is taking cooking lessons – as well as guitar, voice and fencing lessons. As somebody recently told Ryder, she is "one diverse babe." She's constantly turning her memorably bizarre dreams (like the one about being dragged around *Mad Max*–style by a truck in the desert, then suddenly sitting next to Melanie Griffith at the Oscars) into short stories and scripts. The script she's sold, written with *Beetlejuice* screenwriter Michael McDowell, is "corny romantic, almost a

satire, about a girl who works in a bobby-pin factory whose dreams come true." Her other hobbies include seeking out and breaking into abandoned houses in the hills – to "tell ghost stories, be mischievous and freak people out" – and driving around with girlfriends, spying on guys they have crushes on, using walkie-talkies.

Though Ryder says she's going to eat only one pancake, she downs two, then grabs her waist and grimaces, saying, "I'm *sooo* full." She skips into her cluttered room and rummages through a disarray of clothing, photos and books for some show and tell. "This is one of my favorite books," she says, waving Colette's *Claudine.* "It's really cheeseball and good."

Then she pulls out an old class picture, dated 1977–78. "Look at that outfit!" Ryder says. "I was such a weirdo, wasn't I?" Second-grader Winona Horowitz has long, dirty blond hair and is wearing a baggy dress over pants, a strange frilly-collared shirt – and a bemused smile.

"Noni wore the most inconsistent get-ups, yet on her they looked great," says her mother, Cindy Horowitz. "She had her own style, which she had no intention of altering." As a kid, Winona would go to San Francisco Giants baseball games wearing a cap of the archrival Dodgers and be quite surprised when rabid fans doused her with beer. "She has a sense of identity that's pure and more self-confident than anyone else in the family, including her father and myself," says Cindy. "I realized it when she was three to four. She went through materials so fast – drawing supplies, toys, books – you had to keep giving her stuff to keep her interested. She'd just consume them."

Ryder's personality is the product of a sort of alternative childhood, similar to the ones enjoyed by such young celebrities as Uma Thurman, River Phoenix and Chynna Phillips. "I see Noni as one of the first members of a new generation," says her godfather, Timothy Leary. "The Kids of the Summer of Love."

Her parents, Leary says, are "hippie intellectuals and psychedelic scholars." Cindy went to San Francisco in 1965 with her first husband and participated in the first be-in, then discovered Buddhism, macrobiotics and Aldous Huxley's utopian ideals. (Winona has two half siblings from that marriage: a sister, Sunyata, twenty-one, whose name comes from the Tibetan *Book of the Dead,* and a brother, Jubal, nineteen, whose name came to Cindy in a dream. She also has a thirteen-year-old brother, Uri.) In 1970, Cindy married Michael Horowitz, a book antiquarian who was Leary's archivist.

In October 1971, Winona was born near Winona, Minnesota. Soon after, the family returned to San Francisco, sharing a house in the Haight with Cindy's ex and his second wife. Winona toddled around the Zen preschool or hung around while her father drank coffee at the Cafe Trieste with Allen Ginsberg. During these years, her parents were editing books: *Moksha,* about the psychedelic, visionary experiences of Aldous Huxley; and *Shaman Woman, Mainline Lady,* about the transcendental discoveries of women from Cleopatra to Patti Smith. (Today, in addition to managing Winona's career, Cindy runs a video-production company; Michael runs Flashback Books, specializing in counterculture writings.)

"My parents know what it's like to, like, take a drug and

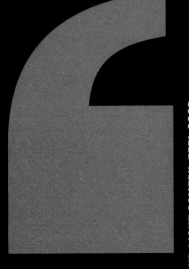

SHE IS VERY, VERY DETERMINED. AROUND THE SET SHE GIGGLES LIKE SOMEONE WHO HAS JUST COME OUT OF HIGH SCHOOL. BUT WHEN THE CAMERA ROLLS, SHE DOESN'T SCREW AROUND.
RICHARD E. GRANT, 'DRACULA' AND 'THE AGE OF INNOCENCE' COSTAR, 1997

NONI WAS OFFERED NINE-THOUSAND LIGHT-COMEDY, FEEL-GOOD, HITS-OF-THE-SUMMER MOVIES, AND SHE CHOSE ONE WHERE SHE KILLS ALL HER FRIENDS. SHE'S A PURE-AT-HEART PERSON WHO KNOWS THAT THE DARKNESS IS ALL AROUND HER. SHE BRINGS TO LIGHT THAT THERE IS TRUTH AND LOVE EVEN IN THE DARKEST IMPULSES. ROBERT DOWNEY JR., '1969' COSTAR, MAY 1989

SHE WAS SITTING THERE IN A WHITE SATIN DRESS, SIPPING A COKE. I THOUGHT, "WOW, WHAT AN INCREDIBLE BEAUTY." IT'S SOMETHING ABOUT HER EYES. SHE'S RADIANT.
BRUCE DAVISON, 'THE CRUCIBLE' COSTAR, JANUARY 1997

KURT IS LEAVING

WE HAD A GOOD TIME FILMING ['DRACULA']. I FELT LIKE DAD ON THE FILM. I WOULD DO MY HANNIBAL LECTER FOR WINONA; SHE ENJOYED THAT.
'DRACULA' COSTAR ANTHONY HOPKINS, NOVEMBER 1992

IT'S AMAZING. SHE'LL JUST CALL ME UP AND SAY, "I WROTE ANOTHER SCRIPT," LIKE "I DID ANOTHER LOAD OF LAUNDRY." TO ME, THAT'S LIKE BENCH-PRESSING THE SEARS TOWER.
ROBERT DOWNEY JR., MAY 1989

DIRECTOR AND 'LUCAS' CASTING DIRECTOR DAVID SELTZER, MAY 1989 HER MOUTH WAS BEING CONTRADICTED BY THE EYES. INNER LIFE. WHATEVER MESSAGE WAS BEING SAID BY HAD THE KIND OF PRESENCE I HAD NEVER SEEN — AN THERE WAS WINONA, THIS LITTLE FRAIL BIRD. SHE

IT'S TOUGH NOT TO BRING YOUR FRIENDS INTO YOUR MUSIC SOMETIMES, SO THERE'S THIS LYRIC IN A SONG THAT I KIND OF CHANGED. IT GOES, "I'VE BEEN TO MINNESOTA / I'VE BEEN TO ARIZONA / OH, LORD, YOU KNOW, I'VE BEEN TO WINONA."
DAVE PIRNER OF SOUL ASYLUM, JUNE 1995

IN HER TEENS, SHE OFFERED SOMETHING NOBODY ELSE COULD, AND SHE'LL DO THAT IN HER ADULT ROLES. I'M NOT WORRIED ABOUT WINONA. SHE'LL DO JUST FINE.
'BEETLEJUICE' AND 'EDWARD SCISSORHANDS' DIRECTOR TIM BURTON, JANUARY 1991

HER APPEAL ISN'T HARD TO FIGURE OUT — SHE'S A BRILLIANT ACTRESS. WHEN SHE DOES A ROLE, SHE'S BRILLIANT. AUDIENCES LOVE TO WATCH HER.
TOM SHERAK, CHAIRMAN OF TWENTIETH CENTURY FOX, DOMESTIC FILMS, MARCH 1997

I'LL TEASE HER THAT SHE'S LIKE A LITTLE WITCH. HER INSTINCTS ARE SO GOOD IT'S ALMOST CREEPY. FROM HER FIRST FILM TO HER LAST, YOU LOOK AT HER AND SAY, "THERE'S A MOVIE STAR."
PRODUCER DENISE DI NOVI, 1990

A RING COULD FALL DOWN A DRAIN. MY TATTOO WON'T.
JOHNNY DEPP, FEBRUARY 1991

ME FOR WINONA.
COURTNEY LOVE, MARCH 1994

WINONA'S HAVING SUCH A GOOD CAREER BECAUSE SHE NEVER WORRIES ABOUT HER CAREER. SHE DOES WHAT INTERESTS HER RATHER THAN WHAT LOOKS LIKE JUST ANOTHER STEP ON THE HOLLYWOOD CHESSBOARD.
'THE CRUCIBLE' DIRECTOR NICHOLAS HYTNER, DECEMBER 1996

SHE HAS INSTINCTS ABOUT PEOPLE THAT BORDER ON THE PSYCHIC. RYDER MAY MAKE A REPORTED $4 MILLION PER PICTURE, BUT SHE'S DOWN TO EARTH.
PRODUCER DENISE DI NOVI, OCTOBER 1995

IT WAS DELIGHTFUL TO WORK WITH SOMEONE AS FINE-TUNED AS SHE IS. IT'S LIKE HAVING THIS MOST PERFECT MUSICAL INSTRUMENT TO PLAY.
'LITTLE WOMEN' DIRECTOR GILLIAN ARMSTRONG, MAY 1995

go out in public and *flip out*," says Winona. "They always said, 'If you ever want to do anything, you just have to tell us about it, and you have to go through us.' "

As a result, Ryder seems unlikely to be a young Hollywood casualty: "Noni's never gonna end up with a cocaine habit!" says Leary. "These kids who've grown up in houses where marijuana was smoked are not going to go berserk the first time a guy in a raincoat offers 'em something in an alley."

When Winona was seven, the Horowitzes left the Haight for a three-hundred-acre Northern California enclave of seven families, which Leary terms "one of the most successful, upscale hippie communes in the country."

"It wasn't as hippie-do as it sounds," says Ryder. "A lot of people, when they hear the word *commune,* connect it with, like, everyone's on acid and running around naked. This was more like this weird suburb, if suburbs were really cool. It was just a bunch of houses on this chunk of land; we had horses and gardens. You have so much freedom, you can go roaming anywhere. We didn't have electricity, which was weird, but it was great to grow up that way. We didn't have TV, so you'd have to *do* stuff. My friends' names were Tatonka, Gulliver and Rio. We'd have hammock contests, sit around and make up stories, make up weird games. I don't know — it was a weird, weird childhood. I mean, it was great."

IT WAS THE LESS-THAN-IDYLLIC aspects of her childhood that propelled Ryder into acting. Because Michael's city job and the older kids' school were too far away, in 1981 the Horowitzes went nuclear, leaving the commune for Petaluma. Winona soon discovered that her close-cropped hair, tomboyish clothes and offbeat interests (she would join Amnesty International at twelve) made her a suburban reject. On her third day at her new junior high, she was standing at her locker when she heard someone say, "Hey, faggot." She turned around and, mistaken for an effeminate boy, was beaten up. Not wanting to return to school, she was put on home study; this quickly bored her, so her parents suggested she take an acting class at San Francisco's prestigious American Conservatory Theatre.

"We weren't thinking of her being professional," says her mother. "We just wanted her to be happy, to be around more imaginative peers."

At ACT, says Ryder "they'd give us these weirdo plays like *The Glass Menagerie,* and there were always these twelve-year-old girls playing these *women.* So I asked if I could find my own monologue to perform. I read from J.D. Salinger's *Franny & Zooey.* I made it like she was sitting, talking to her boyfriend. I had a connection with Salinger-speak; the way she talked made sense. It was the first time that I felt that feeling you get when you're acting — that sort of *yeah!* feeling."

Talent scout Deborah Lucchesi noticed, and she submitted a screen test of Ryder for the movie *Desert Bloom;* Triad Artists saw the videotape and signed Ryder without even meeting her. Director David Seltzer saw the tape when he was casting *Lucas;* after watching seven actresses do the same scene, he suddenly sat up and stared at the screen. "There was Winona," he recalls, "this little frail bird. She had the kind of presence I

had never seen — an inner life. Whatever message was being said by her mouth was being contradicted by the eyes."

Meanwhile, Ryder had reenrolled in public school at Petaluma's other junior high. One day, she remembers, she walked home "like a hundred miles, the longest walk. And I always carried my book bag with the strap around my head. So I walk in the house — I practically had whiplash — and my sister goes, 'Oh, you got the part in that movie.' It was really cool."

IT'S A FEW WEEKS BEFORE *Heathers* opens (to mostly rave reviews), and Ryder and costar Christian Slater, nineteen, are about to appear at a promotional screening at a New York adult-school film class. The mostly suburban, middle-aged audience is clearly troubled by the movie's lighthearted treatment of diabolical themes, and many stalk out midway, muttering epithets like "awful" and "lousy."

Backstage, Ryder is worried — will the audience hate her, too? She gets an idea and whispers it to Slater. When the screening ends, the two actors come out from behind the curtain and sit in chairs onstage, holding hands.

"What, are you nervous?" teacher Ralph Applebaum asks. They look at each other.

"We just got married," says Slater, grinning.

"Last week," Ryder says "in Vegas."

Some class members applaud, others look befuddled. Slater and Ryder never drop the conceit, calling each other "honey," and their charm overpowers their critics.

A few days later Ryder is striding briskly through Central Park wearing Slater's leather biker jacket; the zipper won't zip, so her hands clasp it shut against the chilly spring breeze. She laughingly recalls the idea of marrying Slater. "We talked about how we were going to do all the Hollywood marriage things," she says, "like stage fights in restaurants, be really reclusive but then leak out everything; he'd cover my face when photographers came, like Sean and Madonna."

But after Slater went on a TV talk show and proposed to her on the air, Ryder suddenly tired of the joke. "People have been calling me about it," she says. "It doesn't sound too good. Marriage would be fun, but I don't think I'm ready for it yet."

The funny thing is, Slater *did* fall in love with Ryder. He and the actress playing the lead Heather, Kim Walker, had been dating for a couple of years when *Heathers* started shooting. "We never fooled around or anything during the movie," Ryder says. But after the filming, Slater broke up with Walker and started dating Ryder.

"It was only for a couple of weeks," Ryder says. "It was too weird. You know, when you're really good friends with somebody? It's hard when you *try* to make something work. It's bogus. It should just happen naturally."

She plays idly with a silver ring on her middle finger. She says that it's an Irish claddagh ring, signifying love, friendship and loyalty; wearing it with its small crown pointing up means she's "taken." Currently, she's wearing the crown down. The longest relationship she's had, six months, ended because she was away on movie shoots all the time.

"I don't have a lot of time for that kind of stuff," she says, "which is a drag, but it's almost a blessing in disguise." She does note that since she finished *Heathers,* "I'm taking more of an interest in the way I look. I actually became a little more feminine. Before, I just dressed *however.* I'd go to the set in my pajamas."

Heathers had another effect. "It taught me a lot about what I want to do with my life, my career," Ryder says. "Which is never do anything I don't feel 100 percent about. I don't have any big floor plan, but I wouldn't do a movie where I thought I'd influence anybody in a bad way.

"Having people look up to me freaks me out," she says. "It's actually motivating, because it makes me want to do a really good job. But what if I do something really stupid? That could, like, shatter somebody's image of me. So I don't have the freedom to do really stupid things." She realizes what she's saying and cackles. "Which *is* what I'm striving for!"

Ryder takes a seat on a park bench and stares out at the rowing pond. She suddenly looks tired. She's been doing *Heathers* promotions for a few weeks' running – this morning waking up at dawn to do the *Today* show – and her fame seems finally to be taking its toll. "I haven't been remembering my dreams," she says, "because I'm so stressed and not sleeping at all. It's awful. I might stop for good."

The filming of *Welcome Home, Roxy Carmichael* will be starting soon – she's already wearing Dinky's ID bracelet – and she will have to postpone the car trip she'd been planning with her friend Heather. "We were gonna do a Jack Kerouac *On the Road* thing," Ryder says, "go across the country in a big boat, write really bad poetry. I want to get all that stuff out of the way so I won't resent college at all, like it's stealing my life away." (She says she wants to go somewhere "mellow" on the East Coast with Heather, who today is off modeling in Japan; neither of them has been in a formal classroom since midway through tenth grade.)

"A lot of people ask me if I'm missing out on anything," she says. "I don't think so. Sometimes I'll be talking to Helene, this friend back in Petaluma who's still in high school, and I'll think, 'God, it would be so fun to be like Helene, being on the track team and going to the Valentine's dance and stuff like that.' But then I realize that I don't really have it in me to enjoy the social thing. I was always one of the geeks."

The shadows grow longer as the afternoon winds down, and feeling chilled, Ryder gets up from the bench to head back to her hotel. "I was going to fly out of here on the nineteenth," she says, "but that was the day Randy Rhoads [Ozzy Osbourne's guitarist] died in a plane crash. I try to avoid flying then. I know some day I'll have to, and it'll flip me out."

The cold air has gotten to her, and now her nose has begun to run. "Do you have a handkerchief I could borrow?" she asks. "It's okay – it's just little-girl snot."

L AST NIGHT I DECIDED," Winona Ryder says. "I'm moving. Getting *out* of L.A." Her phone voice is frazzled, but her resolve sounds firm. It's the night of the Academy Awards, and she's in her apartment waiting for Slater to pick her up in a limo.

The source of her new vexation is, again, gossip. "Last night this friend called me on the phone and told me there were these *other* rumors about me, and I *flipped out,"* she says. "I *hate* it when you can't clear something up. I must be such a wimp. I think I'm gonna find a cottage somewhere. Maybe New Orleans. Or I'm going to college, like, *soon.* Of course, you have to apply, don't you?"

She never did find an Oscar dress, so she's ended up wearing her roommate's black sequined miniskirt, black high heels and red lipstick. "I look very Sixties," she says. "I'm wearing, like, eight pairs of stockings 'cause I don't want to get a run."

She cheers up when she remembers the review of *Heathers* in this week's *Village Voice.* "This is going to sound really obnoxious," she says. "But listen to what it says: 'Winona Ryder plays the conflicted Veronica with deeper-than-method conviction.' That's good, isn't it?"

The limo honks outside. "Oh, wait!" she cries. "Should I bring a jacket? Ohmigod, should I bring a purse? What will I keep my lipstick in?" She hangs up midcrisis. *Que será, será.* **W**

{ R E V I E W S }

WeLcome Home, ROXY carmicHaeL

Rolling Stone, *November 1, 1990*

W INONA RYDER EXCELS as a small-town teen who thinks the celebrity returning home after many years is her real mother. The film makes an effort to show the destructiveness of hero worship but soon dissolves into TV pap. *~Peter Travers*

mermaiDs

Rolling Stone, *January 10, 1991*

S ET IN MASSACHUSETTS in 1963, this period piece tells the kind of parent-teen-conflict story that sank Bette Midler's soapy *Stella.* And Richard Benjamin's direction is, to put it kindly, perfunctory. But Cher and Winona Ryder, playing the mother and daughter (Christina Ricci is the younger daughter), make this moonbeam of a comedy lively and affecting. Cher invests her divorcee character with a gutsy integrity, and the luminous Ryder again shows why she's one of the finest young actresses in movies. The irrepressible Bob Hoskins also turns up as Cher's unlikely new boyfriend. So even if the fluff gets to be too much, you're in good company. *~Peter Travers*

EDWARD SCISSORHANDS

Rolling Stone, *January 10, 1991*

DIRECTOR TIM BURTON'S richly entertaining update of the Frankenstein story is the year's most comic, romantic and haunting film fantasy. The title character, played with touching gravity by Johnny Depp, is the handiwork of an aging inventor – Vincent Price, in a lovely cameo – who lives in a dark, musty mansion overlooking a small town of pastel-colored tract houses (exteriors were shot in Florida). Engaged in fanciful cooking experiments, the lonely inventor turns one of his cookie-cutting machines into a boy, a companion to chat with and instruct in the wonders of art, poetry and etiquette. But just before he can provide Edward with hands instead of shears, the inventor dies, leaving his synthetic son alone in a world he knows only from the old magazine clippings he keeps near his bed of straw.

Enter Avon lady Peg Boggs (Dianne Wiest, using her sunny squint to fine advantage), who has wandered off her usual route. Peg is alarmed at first by the flash of Edward's lethal blades. But her maternal instincts are soon aroused. Edward is a hazard, slicing gashes in his chalky face every time he wipes away a stray hair. This benign Freddy Krueger (ironically, Depp appeared as a victim in *Nightmare on Elm Street)* presents a make-over challenge even for Avon.

Peg does more than suggest a good astringent, she takes him home to her husband, Bill (a marvelously wry Alan Arkin), and their children, Kevin (Robert Oliveri) and Kim (Winona Ryder). Edward is struck by the family photographs, especially of blond cheerleader Kim. With scant dialogue, Depp artfully expresses the fierce longing in gentle Edward; it's a terrific performance.

For a while Burton and screenwriter Caroline Thompson have fun showing Edward's struggles to get dressed, use silverware and sleep in a water bed without wreaking havoc. Production designer Bo Welch (*Beetlejuice*) has fashioned sets that look like a garish John Waters nightmare of Fifties suburbia with a Nineties twist. It's Edward who eradicates the blandness by sculpting the town's hedges into exotic topiaries of animals and people. He gives elaborate haircuts to the neighborhood dogs and then moves on to their owners. Edward is a sensation.

As in Burton's other films (*Pee-wee's Big Adventure, Beetlejuice* and *Batman),* the outsider soon becomes the outcast, and the laughs are soon tinged with melancholy. Burton, a misfit kid from California who took solace in drawing cartoons and watching Vincent Price horror movies, clearly relates personally to Edward's situation. Burton shows how the townspeople's curiosity about Edward turns to suspicion and hostility (not unlike Hollywood's reaction to an innovative mind). Edward is denounced as a freak, a fake, a demon. An oversexed housewife (a ripely funny Kathy Baker) tries to seduce him. A hissable teen bully (Anthony Michael Hall) forces him into crime and violence. And when Edward tries to comfort those he loves, his touch draws blood.

Burton's flamboyant style courts disaster and sometimes achieves it. A few scenes are clumsily staged; a few others are fussy beyond endurance. But Burton is a true movie visionary with uncommon insights into hearts in torment. Kim is initially disgusted at the notion of holding Edward's hand. "Picture the damage he could do other places," says one of her friends. But Kim comes to cherish Edward for his imagination and devotion. He creates ice sculptures while she dances in the flakes to Danny Elfman's engulfing score. It's a cathartic moment – the artist sharing his feelings through his art. Depp and Ryder, a gifted actress, give the potentially sappy scene a potent intimacy. Later, when Kim reaches out to Edward, he pulls back his sharp, cold hands in despair until she tenderly wraps her arms around his chest. The memory of that moment suffuses the film even at the somber climax, which recalls Batman's poignant solitude atop that Gotham City tower. *Edward Scissorhands* isn't perfect. It's something better: pure magic. ~ *Peter Travers*

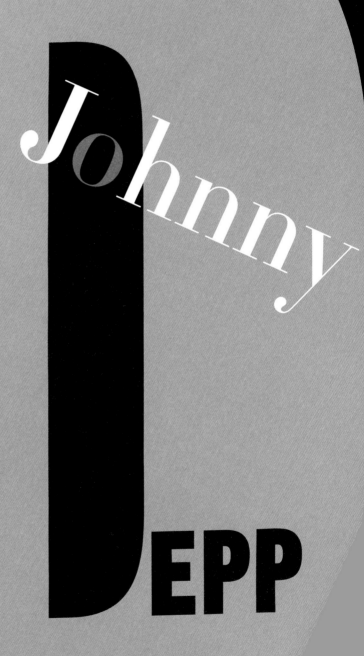

{ By Bill Zehme }

SWEET SENSATION

Rolling Stone, *January 10, 1991*

He was born Depp. He has always been Depp. As a boy, he was ridiculed for it. In the schoolyard, he was called Dipp. Or Deppity Dawg. Later he was called Johnny Deeper, this based upon a popular adolescent joke he barely remembers: "Something about some guy having sex with some girl who kept saying, 'Johnny, deeper!' " He conjures up this dark memory with visible embarrassment. Being Depp, you see, has never been easy.

Depp came into my life during his Hollywood years, a time when the Depp name had begun to really stand for something. The day we met, he extended his hand to shake mine, except that his hand was not a hand so much as it was weaponry. In place of fingers, there were blades. This was the sort of unpredictability I would later come to expect from Depp. At the moment, however, we were on a Twentieth Century Fox soundstage where he was making *Edward Scissorhands,* his second major film, in which he portrayed the man-made boy with scissors for fingers. He laughed quietly at his own comic gesture and then introduced me to his attorneys, who hovered nearby. (Depp is a master of the ironic nuance.) Soon he was asking me what I knew of Al Capone and doing his impersonation of Warren Beatty blinking. Such is the irrepressible spirit of Depp.

Now I will reveal all that I know of Johnny Depp. I will tell of our adventures together: the time we found Jesus, or a guy who said he was Jesus, on Santa Monica Boulevard and Depp gave him cigarettes. The time we ate eggs with his movie-star fiancée, Winona Ryder, whom he loves profoundly. The time we trespassed on Harry Houdini's abandoned property in the Hollywood Hills and got yelled at. I will describe his tattoos, his problem facial hair, his recurring nightmares that feature the Skipper from *Gilligan's Island.* Clearly, earlier biographers have never gotten much of the real Depp, focusing instead on the surface Depp. This, then, is an all-new Depp – a man who lives hard, loves hard, but most of all, thinks hard.

The days I knew Depp best came and went quickly. There were three of them in all. They were November days, as I recall. The first one began in a coffee shop, as so many

things do in the life of John Christopher Depp II. Winona had left him that day. Left him at the coffee shop. Then she drove off to do some errands. So he was very much alone. He was smoking too much and drinking too much coffee, but who could blame him? He said he was enslaved by caffeine and nicotine and didn't sound proud of it. "I like to be pumped up and hacking phlegm at the same time," he said wryly.

"Coupla tequila worms flying out here and there," Depp said, but he was joking about that. He hadn't touched the hard stuff for a solid month, maybe longer. Depp was as dry as he'd ever been in all of his twenty-seven years.

Nobody recognized Depp in public places, not when I was with him. He is a man of the people and therefore doesn't stand out much. Yes, he continues to be a teen idol and a heartthrob ("a throbbing thing," he calls himself), but frankly he looks like someone else. Director John Waters, who cast Depp as a delinquent greaseball in the film *Cry-Baby,* used to imagine him as "the best looking gas-station attendant who ever lived." Or as Waters later told me appreciatively, "Johnny could play a wonderfully sexy mass murderer. I mean, it is a part *made* for him." Which is to say, there is a shadiness to Depp. He looks attractively unwashed. ("Nobody looks better in rags," said Waters of the basic Depp sartorial statement.) As such, he does not possess the burden of great presence. He speaks and moves with quiet dignity. You hardly know he is there. It is easy to sit in silence with him, although ultimately – and I think he would agree here – not very interesting.

If Depp is anything, he is interesting. He takes the big risks. Tom Cruise, the rumor goes, wanted to play the role of tragic, disfigured Edward Scissorhands – but only if his face was cosmetically restored by picture's end. Not Depp. He wore Edward's scars like medals. And he wore the unwieldy, imposing hand shears with brio, recognizing the lyric poetry in Edward's fateful curse. (Edward, who cannot touch anything without slashing it, is a metaphor for the outsider in all of us, including Depp, who knows what it's like to be mocked for being a little different. He is, after all, a teen idol.) "He certainly was closest to the image of the character," said Tim Burton, who directed Depp in *Edward* and Jack Nicholson in *Batman* and Michael Keaton in *Beetlejuice* and Pee-wee Herman in *Pee-wee's Big Adventure,* as well as many other actors in those same movies. "Like Edward, Johnny really is perceived as something he is not. Before we met, I'd certainly read about him as the Difficult Heartthrob. But you look at him and you get a feeling. There is a lot of pain and humor and darkness and light. I think for him [the role] is probably very personal. It's just a very strong internal feeling of loneliness. It's not something he talks about or even can talk about, because it's sad, ya know. What are ya gonna do?"

If you are Depp, you do what you can. Indeed, so devoted to Edward's metaphoric millstone was he that, when smoking off camera, Depp stoically learned to hold his cigarettes between the scissors' blades. During shooting days in Florida, when temperatures soared above 110 degrees, he stayed trussed up in Edward's black leather bodysuit without complaint. "I would freak out," said Winona, who played Edward's dream girl in the film, "just thinking of how he must feel, like if he had an itch or if he had to go to the bathroom. . . ." But Depp, being Depp, simply suffered in silence and dramatically cut down on his coffee intake. He learned to ignore his bladder and thus diminish the likelihood of horrible self-inflicted wounds. It was no wonder, really, that his performance demonstrated such admirable restraint. "I had to just sort of deal with it," he would say later, a better man for having endured his craft.

"If there's any movie in the history of the entire world, and even in the history of any literature," Depp said triumphantly, "*Edward Scissorhands* was the movie I would want to do. And I fuckin' did it. When I first saw it, I was scared, because I kept thinking, 'God, I just can't believe I did this fuckin' movie.'"

But then Depp is an impassioned, if unlikely, aesthete, a bedraggled *literateur* of sorts. He is a high school dropout with a lust for first editions. Once I saw him pay $75 for a rare Hemingway as if it were a pack of Marlboros, and I noticed the swagger in his stride when he carried the book off. He cites Jack Kerouac and J.D. Salinger, two idols, with staggering frequency. His most prized possession – and one that cost him a good portion of his burgeoning fortune – is a book on black culture in whose margins Kerouac has scribbled and doodled. "It's a piece of history," he told me reverently. "I look at it every day."

And then there is fine art:

"Gacy!" Depp said excitedly, in reference to imprisoned mass murderer John Wayne Gacy. There, in our coffee shop, I had handed him an order form listing Gacy's latest oil paintings, knowing that Depp was the owner of a Gacy clown portrait. (Depp, incidentally, lives in mortal fear of clowns.) "The *Hi Ho Series!*" he exclaimed, impressed. "Shit!" He perused the form, shuddered, then told me that he'd gotten rid of his Gacy canvas. "When I got it, I heard the money was going to the families of the victims," he said, but later he suspected otherwise. "The paintings are really scary and weird and great, but I don't want to contribute to something as evil as that."

We went walking that evening. Depp likes to walk. "It's good butt exercise," he told me. "It's good for the rump." Depp, it turns out, has no car. He does have a broken truck. For a long time, he had no home. He and Winona moved from hotel to hotel until they recently got a place in Beverly Hills. They did share a loft in New York for a brief time, but they tired of the East. So they came West, where no one walks except Depp (whenever Winona is using their rental car, that is). But even on foot, Depp is like a dedicated motorist, ever vigilant of traffic minutiae. "Your seat belt! Your seat belt!" he hollered into the snarl of Beverly Boulevard, where we trod along. Depp had spotted a man driving with his seat belt dragging out on the pavement and could not bear to think of the consequences. The startled driver now owes his life to Depp. Likewise, Depp spotted a woman driving with her door ajar. "Your door!" he yelled. "Your door is open!" No doubt, that very woman is now living a rich and productive life, thanks to the selfless instincts of a certain movie actor who is currently looking carefully for his next big project.

Once, when he was very young, Depp harbored an irrational fear of John Davidson, the great musical entertainer. Today Depp has conquered that fear and, in fact, even appeared in a major motion picture with Davidson. (In *Edward Scissorhands,* Davidson convincingly played a talk-show host who interviews Depp, as Edward.) "He was a really sweet guy," said Depp magnanimously. "I felt bad for ever being scared of him." So imagine Depp's reaction when we purchased a map to the stars' homes from a street peddler, and the very first address he saw was Davidson's. "Ooooooh – John Davidson!" he crowed, reading off the numbers and displaying no residue of unexorcised terror. This was one cured customer. (Of course, we never went to Davidson's house. We didn't go to anyone's house – not to Peter Falk's or Sandy Koufax's or Phyllis Diller's or Anna Marie Alberghetti's. We were, after all, on foot.)

Instead, we wandered aimlessly, and he spoke of his darkest visions. "The most disturbing dream I ever had," Depp said, "and I hope this is taken the right way, because I'm sure he was a very sweet man – was one where Alan Hale Jr., the Skipper [on *Gilligan's Island*], was chasing me. He was in his wardrobe from the show – the white cap and white pants and everything, and I was running from him. He got on a bicycle and chased me into this weird little apartment, really small, very low rent. I looked over to my right, and there was an elderly woman, ethnic looking, squatting. She raised up her muumuu and took a piss. I got the fuck out of there immediately, because she was very evil. Then I remember diving over the bushes, where the Skipper was trying to get me, and then I woke up."

By now, the origins of Depp are familiar to most functioning Americans.

Born in Owensboro, Kentucky, the self-styled barbecue capital of the world, Depp was the fourth child of John Depp, a city engineer, and his wife, Betty Sue, a waitress at many fine coffee shops. (Her famous son would later have her name tattooed above his left bicep, so as to balance the Indian chief tattooed on his right one, a talisman of his partial Cherokee bloodline.) Depp was a small boy, so early on he learned to rely on his fists, especially when fighting. Eventually, his family settled in Miramar, Florida, and Depp, seven at the time, elected to go with them.

Rebellious in school, he was once suspended for mooning a gym teacher. He learned to smoke by age twelve and then drink and finally take drugs. By fourteen, however, he is said to have sworn off drugs forever. Two years later, his parents divorced, and soon after, Depp quit high school to join a rock band called the Kids, who became a local sensation and opening act for the likes of Talking Heads, the B-52's and Iggy Pop. (He remembers that his first words to Iggy Pop, one of his heroes and later a friend, were, inexplicably, "Fuck you, fuck you, fuck you." In response, a perplexed Pop called him a "little turd.")

At twenty, he married Lori Anne Allison, a musician and relative of a band mate, and together (band included) they left Florida for Hollywood, where the Kids broke up and so did Depp and Lori. Alone and starving, Depp turned to acting and made his screen debut in the original *Nightmare on Elm Street* as a guy swallowed by a bed. (Grateful to this day for that break, Depp graciously will appear in the next *Elm Street* sequel as a cameo murder victim.) Then came *Platoon,* in which Depp played an interpreter who dies off-camera. But his movie career would have to wait: Depp next became, for four years, America's favorite boy detective.

He was undercover high school cop Tom Hanson on Fox's *21 Jump Street,* a television series Depp hated and never saw more than six episodes of. Still, it transformed him into the major show-business figure he is today, and better yet, the babes loved him. Beautiful actresses flocked to his side. Before it was over, there were two failed engagements: to Sherilyn Fenn (*Twin Peaks*) and to Jennifer Grey (*Dirty Dancing*). Then the TV show was canceled. But by now John Waters had hired him to star as the misunderstood hood Cry-Baby Walker – his first big-screen lead role! – in the troubled-teen musical *Cry-Baby* that was released in April 1990. And it was during this time that he met Winona Ryder, the girl who would change his life forever.

On my second day with Depp, Winona Ryder

showed up. She is nineteen and all pluck, the thinking man's actress for her generation. Depp is the thinking man who thinks of her most. He swells in her presence. When they hug, they hug fiercely, in focused silence; their squeeze keeps re-grouping. They seem to be lost in each other. She smokes his cigarettes, and she is not a smoker. ("You're on the filter, babe," he will coach her.)

Hands locked, they descended upon Barney's Beanery, a frequent haunt, for caffeine, which they now took in desperate helpings. She wore a Tom Waits T-shirt and Depp's engagement ring. She was saying, "I'd never seen anyone get a tattoo before, so I was pretty squeamish, I guess." Depp chuckled and said, "She kept taking the bandage off and staring at it afterwards." They were speaking of WINONA FOREVER, the third and final (for now) Depp tattoo, eternally

etched onto his epidermis: locus, right shoulder. (Depp told me he plans to have his tattoos pickled after his death as keepsakes for his children, should there be any.) This one was carved on at a nearby tattoo parlor as Winona watched with awe. "I sort of was in shock," she said. "I kept thinking it was going to wash off or something. I couldn't believe it was real." Her eyes widened. "I mean, it's a big thing, because *it's so permanent!*"

"It ain't goin' nowhere," Depp said, and by this I knew he meant business. Over hash and eggs, they then traced the history of their romance for me: He knew her work (*Beetlejuice, Heathers*), and she knew his, but they did not know each other. At the première of *Great Balls of Fire!,* a film in which she played Jerry Lee Lewis's child bride, they spotted each other from across the lobby. "I was getting a Coke," Ryder said. "It was a classic glance," he said, "like the zoom lenses in *West Side Story,* and everything else gets foggy." She said, "It wasn't a long moment, but it was suspended." He said, "I knew then." They did not meet that night. Months later, a mutual friend dragged her to Depp's hotel room at the Chateau Marmont, where John Belushi last drew breath, and this is where they began. "I thought maybe he would be a real jerk," she said. "I didn't know. But he was really, really shy." They knew it was love when they both professed deep feelings for Salinger and the soundtrack of the film *The Mission.* Their first date, a few weeks later, was a party at the Hollywood Hills home of counterculture guru Dr. Timothy Leary, who is her godfather. "We were kinda blessed," said Depp, a Beat disciple. As it happens, Winona's father is an esteemed Beat bookseller in Petaluma, California, where she and Depp weekend often. "My parents really love him a lot," she told me. Depp said: "It could have been easy not to like me. Other people might have just seen tattoos."

Tim Burton calls the couple "kind of an evil version of Tracy and Hepburn." Which is to say, as celebrity couples go, these two are dark, spunky, glamorous and resilient, all requisite traits in this cynical age. For they are beset. Tabloid photographers terrorize them at airports, and tabloid reporters regularly report imaginary squalls and breakups. So he gets angry, and she gets incredulous. Winona: "They try to *trip* me at airports!" Depp: "What's shitty about it is that they feel like you *owe* them! That you should stop dead in your tracks and let them piss on you!" Winona: "I will say that there *are* some really nice ones." Depp: "A couple of them are real nice." Winona: "But aren't we allowed to be in a bad mood sometimes? Everybody else is."

We found Jesus after lunch. Winona left (took

the car again), and Depp and I stepped out into the daylight, where we saw a miracle. There, on Santa Monica Boulevard, in front of the Beanery, stood a man who looked very much like the Son of God – in pictures at least. He was swaddled in robes, his face was serene, his eyes were benevolent, his hair was long, his beard was crisp, he wore tattered Reeboks and a decent tan. He even seemed some sort of divine, in an approachable street person sort of way. I do not know if Depp is a praying man, but he is, evidently, a closet theologian, if

one is to judge by the adroitness with which he interviewed this hallowed figure. First, perhaps to put the holy man at ease, Depp complimented him on his clothing. (Was Depp considering a dirty linen motif for himself?)

"I have always dressed like this," said the man in a soft, commanding voice. What, Depp inquired, was his name? "Jesus," the man said, although he used the Hispanic pronunciation (*Hay-zoos*). Where had he come from? "Oh, I don't know," he said. "Heaven." His age? "Over forty." Why had he come to Los Angeles? "I'm here for a special occasion." What was the occasion? "I like it here." Where did he like it best? "Beverly Hills." At which point, Depp whispered to me, "Apocalypse. Second Coming. Armageddon."

Suddenly a Hollywood climber – short, with a noisy sport coat, on his way to lunch – accosted Jesus from the side. "Hey, I just wrote a story treatment about a guy who dresses like Christ and wanders the streets," the Hollywood guy said, seeming as earnest as one of his ilk can seem. "Do you have a phone number where you can be reached in case a deal happens?" (He did not notice Depp, who looked pretty mortified.) Jesus regarded the pitch artist wordlessly, but his message was abundantly clear: idiot. Defeated, the guy slunk away. Said Jesus, "He was different, huh?"

"You want a cigarette for the road?" Depp asked him. Jesus assented, and together the robed one and the young actor smoked for a while. "Take the pack," Depp told him. "I can buy some more." Afterward, Depp seemed thrilled. "I smoked with Christ!" he said, not a little boastfully. "Jesus is a Marlboro man!"

Perhaps it was the brush with Jesus that did it, but Depp spoke to me from his heart that night. He seemed somehow inspired by the divine fellow. "I wish I could grow more facial hair," he said, bemoaning the wispiness of his whiskers. "I can only get an Oriental sort of beard." Spooning up corn chowder in a tiny restaurant, he was openly penitent about his "younger, hellion, hitting-the-sauce kind of days." He owned up to his short fuse: "I've got a bit of a temper." He spoke of a tussle or two and of the circumstances surrounding his arrest in Vancouver during his *21 Jump Street* tenure. Apparently, he tried to visit some friends late one night in their hotel, where Depp himself had once lived, and a security guard would have none of it. "The guy had a boner for me," Depp said. "He had a wild hair up his ass, and he got real mouthy with me, saying, 'I know who you are, but you can't come up unless you're a guest here.' The mistake he eventually made was to put his hands on me. I pushed him back, and then we sort of wrestled around a bit, and I ended up spittin' in his face."

The police didn't want to hear Depp's story. He was jailed for a night, fingerprinted, posed for mug shots ("I wish I could have them"), and in the morning he walked.

But the most beloved legends of Depp are not violent legends. Hardly. For Depp is a name synonymous with great romance. In his young life, he has asked for the troth of four separate women. Whereas other actors are elusive Lotharios, Depp is the marrying kind, unintimidated by the notion of connubial permanence. (Is he trying to succeed where his parents did not?) "I knew this was gonna come up," he said, looking stricken. But Depp is nothing if not courageous. So, for the first time ever in recorded media, he offered these assorted insights into his mythic ardor: "I've never been one of those guys who goes out and screws everything that's in front of him. . . . When you're growing up, you go through a series of misjudgments. Not bad choices, but wrong choices. . . . You know, people make mistakes. We all fuck up. . . . I was really young for the longest time. We were young. {My relationships} weren't as heavy as people think they were. I don't know what it is, possibly I was trying to rectify my family's situation or I was just madly in love. . . .You're the first person that I've talked to about this kind of stuff. And I'm being really honest with you when I say that there's been nothing ever throughout my twenty-seven years that's comparable to the feeling I have with Winona. . . . It's like this weird, bounding atom or something. You can think something is the real thing, but it's different when you feel it. The truth is very powerful. Now I know. Believe me, this WINONA FOREVER tattoo is not something I took lightly. . . . Her eyes kill me."

He then said this about his engagement to Winona: "People don't realize this, but we've been together almost a year and a half. Out of any, whatever, *thing* I've been through before, it hasn't been this long. It wasn't like, 'Hi, nice to meet you, here's a ring.' It was about five months {before we got engaged}. They thought we ran away to Las Vegas and got married." When will their nuptials actually transpire? "The wedding thing?" he said. "We're just gonna do it when we both have time, because we both know we're gonna end up working in the next couple of months. And we want to be able to do it when we can get hitched and then go away for a few months. Leave the country, just go wandering around and be on a beach somewhere with tropical drinks.

"I've never actually come out and said this," Depp added portentously, "but the one claim to fame I'm most proud of is that I'm responsible for having John Waters ordained. I sent in to the Universal Life Church and had him ordained by mail. He's now Reverend John Waters, and we want John to perform the ceremony. Who better? You know what I mean? John is a stand-up guy. And Winona loves the idea."

(From the sanctum of Pastor Waters: "I told them I wouldn't do it without their parents' blessing," said the Reverend. "I mean, I've *met* her parents! They've eaten dinner here! I'm not gonna just horrify them. And of course, I always counsel Johnny and Winona — *too young!* I tell them to *wait, wait, wait!* But I'd be thrilled to perform the ceremony — I'd feel like the pope!")

My last day with Depp went like this: I picked him up at home, which wasn't really home but a small bungalow he and Winona were briefly renting. (Their new house

was not yet inhabitable.) Depp was on the kitchen phone, pacing furiously, caffeine wiring his arteries. Heaps of laundry and luggage and books cluttered the living-room floor. A stray cat was loose in the house. Winona was out. Mail was strewn about. Depp told me about his fan mail, unique in its female pubic hair content — "I've gotten some weird pubes," is how he put it. We got into my car and drove. We passed a slatternly pedestrian. "That," said Depp, "was a man in drag." Depp cannot be fooled.

We passed a coffee shop adorned with a giant rooster. "I have one of those," he said, meaning the rooster. "I have a nine-foot rooster. I have the biggest cock in Los Angeles. My large cock is in storage."

This was the old Depp, spry and antic as ever. He saw a dog and said, coincidentally, that he based his Edward Scissorhands performance on a dog. "He had this unconditional love," said Depp, who probably cherishes that role above any other in the Depp repertoire. "He was this totally pure, completely open character, the sweetest thing in the world, whose appearance is incredibly dangerous — until you get a look at his eyes. I missed Edward when I was done. I really miss him."

We drove to Harry Houdini's house, which wasn't really a house but a scattering of ruins perched above Laurel Canyon. Houdini's ruins, they say, are haunted. Depp read from a guide book, "Nearby Canyon residents tell of strange happenings on the hilltop site." Depp, incidentally, believes that he was once Houdini. "I often think I might have been Houdini at one time," he said. So we dropped over to see if anything looked familiar to him. We scaled a steep hill and found a crumbling staircase and little else. "There's no house," said Depp, disappointed. He was now obviously soured on the whole endeavor. "I bet this was a really romantic place at night," he added dreamily. Then a German woman emerged from a nearby house and, apparently mistaking us for urban archaeologists, chased us off. "Yes, ma'am," said Depp politely as we fled.

Here is how I will remember Depp best: After the Houdini incident, he grew more and more quixotic, thirsting for the wondrous possibilities that lay before him. We snaked through the Hollywood Hills, whose ripened lore endlessly enchants Depp. "I would love to buy Bela Lugosi's old house," he said. "Or Errol Flynn's. Or Charlie Chaplin's. I want some old, depressing history to call my own. Plus, I love the idea of a view." He sat in silent reverie, but within moments was overtaken with purpose. "I think I just have to have a lot of cash," he said calmly. "I also think I want to be a sheik. I want to be the sheik of Hollywood. What do you have to do to become a sheik, anyway? I wonder if it just takes cash. . . ."

Before any further grandiosity could delude him, however, Depp made me stop the car. "Something's wrong with that mailbox!" he said, pointing to a blue corner mailbox that seemed to have exploded. "I'll go see what happened." With that, he hurried to assist a U.S. postal worker hunched over the damaged box. I cannot be certain of how Depp managed to help. But now, whenever mail is delivered safely and on time anywhere in this great land, I don't think it would be presumptuous to say that one American did his part. W

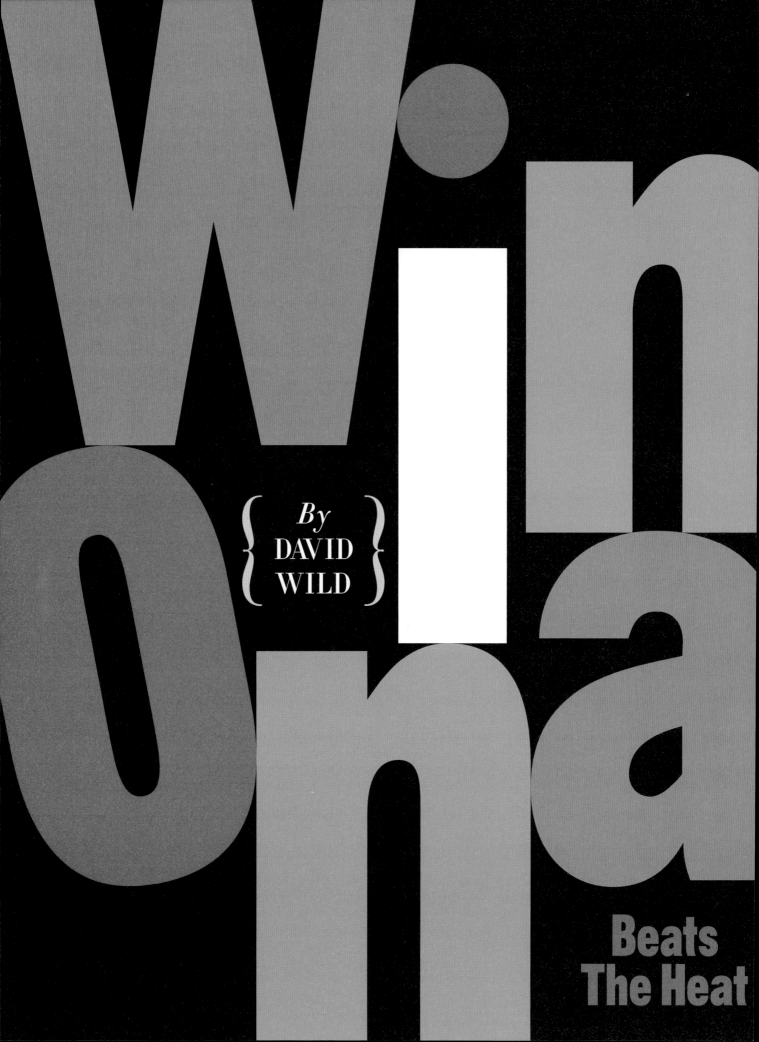

Winona

By
DAVID WILD

Beats
The Heat

THE ORIGINAL 'EDWARD SCISSORHANDS' scissor hands rest peacefully on a wooden chest at the top of the stairs. Among the mementos and messages stuck to the refrigerator are a sweet photo of Johnny Depp with cult director John Waters and a piece of yellow note paper bearing Jason Robards's phone number.

In fact, all around Winona Ryder's recently purchased Los Angeles house, one senses a touching attempt to impose some semblance of domestic normalcy. This home base of Hollywood Hotness 1991 has the relaxed bohemian feel of the actress's native Northern California rather than the standard-issue L.A. glitz. As Ryder passes a room that houses her J.D. Salinger first editions, she apologizes for the unfinished state of the place. "I'm sorry," she says sweetly, "this is the first time I've decorated a home of my own."

Suddenly one realizes that for all her down-to-earth charm, there's actually little that's normal about Winona Ryder and her situation these days. After all, your average nineteen-year-old is not setting up house in this ritzy neighborhood. Your average nineteen-year-old isn't the god-daughter of LSD guru Timothy Leary and didn't attend Black Flag and Agent Orange shows with her dad. Your average nineteen-year-old isn't currently cohabiting with and engaged to Johnny Depp. Your average nineteen-year-old does not have her own production company. And most significant, your average nineteen-year-old is not the single most exciting actress of her generation.

Ryder was born Winona Horowitz in 1971 near Winona, Minnesota. She grew up in the San Francisco area with her bohemian, intellectually inclined parents, Michael and Cindy. Her first role was as Catwoman in a family performance of *Batman.* From there it was on to playing Auntie Em in the summer-workshop production of *The Wizard of Oz* and Willie in *This Property Is Condemned* at the prestigious American Conservatory Theatre. While taking classes at ACT, she was spotted by a talent scout and before long found herself cast in her first movie, *Lucas,* in 1986. Shortly before its release, Winona was asked how she wanted her name to appear in the credits and on a whim chose the last name Ryder. "I think my dad had a Mitch Ryder album on," she says.

Since then, Ryder has made a series of vivid impressions in such films as *Heathers, Beetlejuice, Great Balls of Fire!, Edward Scissorhands* and *Mermaids.* By last year she had become such hot property that she made news not only for films that she starred in but also for one that she didn't: *The Godfather Part III,* which she had to drop out of at the last minute because of physical exhaustion. (She was replaced by the daughter of director Francis Ford Coppola, Sofia).

Despite a résumé that's not exactly jam packed with box-office bonanzas, Ryder is in the enviable position of being able to pick and choose her roles. Recently, she completed work for Jim Jarmusch's still-untitled new film, in which she plays a taxi driver, and she has agreed to appear in Coppola's upcoming remake of *Dracula.* There's also talk of her playing a female Jesus in *The Second Greatest Story Ever Told.*

Ryder says she enjoyed her first brush with widespread media attention around the time of *Heathers* but has grown uncomfortable with talking about herself. "Most interviews of actresses that I read make me want to throw up," she says as she turns off the CD of *Hootenanny,* by her favorite band, the Replacements. "I read one not too long ago in which the actress actually said, 'I really, *really* want to play a blind person.'" She winces and, fine actress that she is, conjures up a convincing gagging noise. With that, Winona Ryder fetches her coffee and cigarettes and prepares to talk.

THIS MAGAZINE NAMED *you Hot Actress in 1989, and things have only gotten warmer since then. What kind of career pressures are on you at this point?*

There's all sorts of pressures on me. But I just ignore strategy and advice in general because I can't listen to anybody but myself. So as a result I've ended up turning down a lot of stuff.

Anything that you regret turning down?

No. Not at all. Sometimes people would tell me: "Oh, you *have* to do this. This picture is going to be really, really *huge.*" And maybe it *was* huge, but I'm not going to do anything for that reason. There are people in Hollywood who devise these entire theories – you can do *two* small movies, but then you *have* to do a big movie. And then you can take meetings for a small movie, but then you really have to do two *really* big movies.

There were people who got on their knees and *begged* me not to do *Heathers.* They told me it was going to ruin my career. All this strategy has nothing to do with creativity or art or acting or any of those things. It has to do with money and power and box office and positioning.

Have you done a movie as a career move?

No, never. I did *1969* because I was sixteen years old, I was really bored, and I wanted to work. And it was a big mistake. But I didn't do the movie because I thought it was going to be some good career move. To a true artist the career stuff shouldn't matter. But it matters to too many of those people who call themselves actors but are really just posers. Some people are in this just because they want to be really rich and they want to have houses everywhere. And that's great. But just don't call yourself an artist and then try to tell everybody that . . . *Road House* was a really powerful, moving movie.

So you don't care about box office?

I'm thrilled if one of my movies is a hit. But you should do what hits you. If I'm in a movie and I'm not really into it, then I feel like I'm . . . *lying* and like maybe other people will pick up on the fact that I'm lying.

The conventional wisdom is that there are no strong roles for women, but this doesn't seem to have been a problem for you.

See, the thing is, that hasn't been a problem for me yet, because I haven't really played any women yet. I've been playing teenagers, and I've been lucky enough to find some pretty good roles. Like, I loved the role of Myra in *Great Balls of Fire!* I really loved the role of Charlotte in *Mermaids,* and I consider Veronica in *Heathers* to be *the* role of my life. Now things get difficult because I've already kind of covered that teenager territory.

Yet you've done so without really appearing in the mainstream teen films. You're one of the few young Americans who have never starred in a John Hughes movie.

Yeah, well, I'm glad of that. That wasn't even an *option* for me. And I don't think he would have ever liked me anyway. Those kinds of films are so corny. I couldn't believe how teenagers didn't mind getting those labels slapped on their backs. God, talk about patronizing. Plus, you watch those movies and everyone is, like, thirty playing eighteen. It's just like "Get a life."

I'm starting to read scripts in which I'd be playing women in their twenties, and I've already found it's more difficult to find a good young-woman role as opposed to a good teenager role. The weirdest thing was when people criticize you about stuff. I did this press junket for *Mermaids* in Aspen, and everyone there was saying, "Why are you *always* playing teenagers?" And, like, I'm *nineteen,* what am I supposed to do – play a judge?

Are you impressed with your young peers in Hollywood?

It's kind of disappointing to see a lot of young actors and actresses. It's like they have a look for everything. They have their *sexy* look, their *angry* look, their *innocent* look. And it's so calculated and so posed. It's such a *poseathon.* Nothing's coming from the inside. It's all exteriors and looks. A lot of the time, I feel some of my peers are in it because they are just really trying to be famous or be looked at. It's not like they really enjoy acting at all. But there are definitely exceptions.

Like who?

I really like Jodie Foster a lot. I think she's going to be just a tremendous director, too. I like Uma Thurman – I think she's a good actress. And I like Julia Roberts.

Considering how quickly things

ON THE SET OF 'EDWARD SCISSORHANDS': DIRECTOR TIM BURTON WITH RYDER IN HER ROLE AS THE BLOND LOVE-INTEREST

happened for you, would a few years of waitressing have made you a better actress?

Some people think that: "She never struggled." So sue me, you know? What do they want? More and more lately, I deal with blatant jealousy. If I were jealous of someone, I wouldn't be blatant about it. People get so strange here. I'm sure people assume I hate Julia Roberts, because she's really hot and gets to do whatever she wants workwise. I like Julia. I know her a little bit, and I think she's a really cool person. So why couldn't I be friends with someone like that? I'm nineteen. I like to know other people around my age. I think she's talented, and I'd rather be losing parts to her than to some idiot.

Why do you think your dropping out of 'Godfather III' caused so much commotion?

I don't know. I'm really burnt out on even defending myself because the truth is so simple. I was sick physically and exhausted. *That's* what happened. It's amazing how people want things to be as complicated and nasty as possible. I think maybe some people are waiting for me to fuck up because I hadn't really fucked up yet.

Obviously, I would have loved to have worked with those wonderful actors and a great director. But it wasn't a *choice.* It wasn't like "Well, I'm not feeling too well today. Maybe I won't do this movie." The doctor was there, and he said: "You have an upper respiratory infection. You can't do it." My leaving the movie was disappointing to everybody, *especially* to me. But Francis Coppola's a father himself. He has a daughter my age – yeah, *obviously* he has a daughter my age – and I think anybody who's a parent could understand. I was seventeen years old, and when you haven't been home for a year and you've been working the whole time and you're *really* sick, you just have to be home. I wanted my mom to bring me soup. People treat me like a kid, and then when they don't want to treat me like a kid, then they treat me like an adult. So they treat me like a kid, and they work me like an adult.

A lot of kids your age are in college. You were a 4.0 student in high school. Have you ever thought of taking a break from acting and going back to school?

Yeah, I've thought about it. But my education hasn't stopped. I read all the time, and I'm still learning. I'm not worried that my IQ is going to drop because I'm not going to college. I really love acting and making movies right now. If I commit to college for four years or even a year, I may have to leave because I get an offer of something I'm dying to do. That's not fair to the school, and it would just screw me up.

And I don't want to knock college, but I went to visit a friend at a college, and I got there and it was like a frat hell or sorority hell or whatever it is called. It felt just like . . .

High school?

Exactly. There were the same sort of obnoxious cliques. It was all the same, just a little bit . . . older.

Did you miss anything by going into acting so young?

I'm not, like, *mourning* the fact that I didn't go to the prom or go to keggers. I don't think I would be doing all that regardless of what I'm doing now.

Being part of a celebrity couple must make it impossible to walk around and not get recognized.

The thing is, living in L.A., we *don't* walk down the street. We just drive cars here. But yeah, it's more so when we're out together, but it's just the price you pay. You get to be rich and famous, and you have got all this money, so you – like, "What are you complaining about?" But the paparazzi can be a nightmare.

Your collective star power has made you two tabloid fodder.

I don't know, because I don't really read those papers. You hear about it. It's like a mosquito; it's annoying, but you can't pay too much attention, because it's too tiresome. I worry about it, then I think anyone with any mind of their own wouldn't be reading that stuff anyway.

I don't even like discussing my relationship with Johnny with the press. It's nobody's business. How do you explain a relationship anyway? Nobody knows anything about it, *nobody,* not even friends know what my relationship is like. I don't even know it. You try to figure out your own feelings and interpret them for yourself, and you have these really strong, incredible, powerful feelings. And then some writer who doesn't know you at all is writing about it. It's like, "Wait, what do you know?"

Is it strange to be – and I'm not sure this is the proper term to use with someone your age – a sex symbol so young?

I don't think it's the right phrase when you're talking about me.

Really? A lot of older men in their twenties and thirties were extremely envious when they heard that I'd be talking to you.

You're kidding.

You don't get a lot of that?

No. A general lack of that, actually. I mean it's *weird.* My friend and her boyfriend had just seen *Mermaids,* and they were, like, saying, "You were *really* sexy in that." I was like, "What?" 'Cause, to me, that was, like, the most unsexy thing I've ever done.

Then what's the most sexy?

I've never done anything deliberately sexy. I'm relatively shy about that stuff. At the same time, it's exciting. But I'm really grateful that I haven't *made* myself on the basis of being sexy. With a lot of actresses, *that's* them. *That's* what they are, *that's* what they're famous for, *that's* what they've sold themselves as. Maybe I've done a couple of bad movies, but I never exploited myself.

Still, you've managed to lose your virginity onscreen a few times already.

Right, in *Great Balls of Fire!* and *Mermaids.* Yes, I've gotten

to share that moment with the world *twice.* I have to say I'm very uncomfortable with scenes like that, because, let's face it, sexuality is such a private thing. Only people in this business have to, you know, *perform* it. But luckily, it's just work, and you don't really – well, there's no *insertion* involved. Thank God. *Thank God.*

As an actress, do you have a specific method?

As an actress, I *hate* to hear actresses talking about their *craft.*

Do you have the desire to do stage work?

Yeah, I know I *should* say yes. But as much as the idea of continuity appeals to me, I think, like, doing the same thing over and over every night would get boring.

If you are really bothered by the concept of doing the same thing every night, then why would you get engaged to Johnny Depp when you are only eighteen?

I'm not going to talk about that . . . I *can't* talk about that, it's too precious. And anyway it's definitely *not* the same thing every night.

Stories about you always comment on your hippie childhood, about growing up on a commune.

And my parents were not these crazy hippies. Maybe my dad was part hippie, but he was more of an intellectual and an observer and a writer. Of course he experimented and did all that stuff people did in the Sixties, but he was, like, on the intellectual side of things. He was doing it all because he was curious, and he recorded it. And I never lived on a commune. For a year we lived in Mendocino in a house with a car, but it was on three hundred acres of land, and there were other houses on the land – it was just tagged as a commune because people wanted to tag it as that. They wanted to make me out as a flower child. But it was an amazing way to grow up.

How so?

My parents are like my best friends, really. It wasn't like they didn't give me any rules. We had this relationship where I could talk to them about things that most kids can't talk to their parents about. I would say: "What's acid like? Everybody is taking acid in my school. What does it do?" And they would say, "Well, you know, this is the bad side of it." They would take all the mystery out of it. They would say: "Well, you know, if you take it and you go to a concert, you are going to get a panic attack and freak out. If you get it on the streets, they make bad, synthetic stuff that's just going to, like, freak you out." So I'd lose interest. Whereas I have a lot of friends who were just told, "*No,* you *can't* do that." And *they're* the ones with the problems now.

Was it ever odd to have such a hip dad?

I remember one time he came to pick me up from school, and he was wearing a SEX PISTOLS T-shirt, and they wouldn't let him pick me up, or they didn't believe he was my dad or something.

You've been written about a lot lately. Any descriptive words you'd like barred from future interviews?

Well, *quirky.* If anyone ever calls me *quirky* again, I think they should be shot.

How about "precocious"?

Well, I'm not precocious, and so I don't know why people call me precocious. Yeah, they should be shot, too. **W**

NIGHT on earTH

US, *June 1992*

I F YOU'VE NEVER SEEN a Jim Jarmusch movie, *Night on Earth* is a great place to start. It's the most accessible, exuberant, free-flowing film he has ever made. For years, Jarmusch has been considered *the* leading independent filmmaker, but by this point, he's outgrown that sometimes patronizing label. He is – clearly and simply – one of America's great directors. Like Woody Allen, Martin Scorsese and very few others, Jarmusch has created a type of movie that is entirely unique. His best films *(Stranger Than Paradise, Mystery Train)* traffic in a completely personal set of paradoxes. They are homegrown yet international, controlled yet improvisational, humane yet invariably hip. In fact, Jarmusch may be the king of cinematic cool.

Like most of Jarmusch's films, *Night on Earth* works off a preset structure. It tells the story of five different cab rides that take place in five different parts of the world (Los Angeles, New York, Paris, Rome, Helsinki). The episodes aren't related by plot so much as time (which always plays a major role in Jarmusch's narratives). In fact, between each chapter, Jarmusch cuts to a wall of clocks that reveal that all five plot lines are taking place simultaneously.

While this clockwork conceit keeps things safely within his cool, cerebral zone, *Night on Earth* generates more energy and belly laughs than one would usually expect. In the past, Jarmusch would risk dead space before he would risk cliché. But here, he even allows himself to lean on some sentimental chestnuts like having the cabbies actually affect their passengers' lives – and vice versa. (I'm not sure if Jarmusch should continue in this more mainstream direction, but

RYDER LOOKING LIKE HER 'NIGHT ON EARTH' CHARAC- TER – A CABBIE CALLED CORKY – WITH HER DIREC- TOR, JIM JARMUSCH, 1991

for the moment, it brings a nice, warm edge to his work.)

Throughout this film, Jarmusch rides a wave of generosity that spills over into the performances. He always gives his actors plenty of space in which to maneuver, but this time out, they seem completely liberated. More than anything else, *Night on Earth* is a miracle of mix-and-match acting styles. It provides a rich, uninhibited display of emotional timbres and incandescent improvisations. In keeping with Jarmusch's hipness, the cast cuts across all boundaries: from the fringe to the mainstream to the foreign film. The short list includes Gena Rowlands, Winona Ryder, Italian comic Roberto Benigni, Giancarlo Esposito, Armin Mueller-Stahl and Rosie Perez. The last three appear in a Manhattan sequence that rises to a precariously high pitch of hilarity. If all of *Night*'s episodes generated such manic magic, Jarmusch may have had his first mall-movie hit (not that he's ever seemed remotely interested in that brand of success).

Considering this movie's bent toward coziness, it might sound like Jarmusch has gone soft. But as the episodic film crosses the globe, *Night on Earth* becomes more dire and downbeat. By the final chilling sequence – featuring a group of men returning home during a cold dawn in Helsinki, Finland – Jarmusch travels back to the silences that give his works their special attraction. Ultimately, *Night on Earth* presents a dense matrix of human possibility. Jarmusch's people pass through the night, finding friction or friendship, sharing secrets or nothing at all. As usual, the director's overhead point of view fuses his fragments into a beautifully neutral statement. There are those who feel that Jarmusch's work requires patience, diligence, perhaps even allegiance. That may be true. But if his films are an acquired taste, it's one well worth developing.   ~ *Lawrence Frascella*

NIGHT ON EARTH

Rolling Stone, *May 14, 1992*

IN A BOX-OFFICE WORLD OF HOT SEX *(Basic Instinct),* hot laughs *(Wayne's World)* and hot shots *(White Men Can't Jump),* the cool comic detachment of Jim Jarmusch is a bracing alternative. Jarmusch offers a hip, urban, brooding take on a pop culture closed off to feeling. In his last film, *Mystery Train,* the filmmaker obliquely observed foreign tourists adrift in the after-hours of Elvis-haunted Memphis. Now, in the lyrically funny and stunningly visualized *Night on Earth,* Jarmusch takes us on five taxi rides in five cities – Los Angeles, New York, Paris, Rome and Helsinki – over the course of a single winter night. The five stories – or puzzle pieces – are linked only by synchronicity and the scrutiny of Jarmusch, who monitors the interaction of drivers and passengers from the alien, but never hostile, perspective of a visitor from another planet.

The film begins in the stars, with the camera looking down on the first story from the darkness. It's past sunset at the L.A. airport (clocks are used throughout the movie to show the time in various countries). Corky (Winona Ryder), a gum-chewing cabdriver who wears army fatigues and layers of attitude, picks up a fare to Beverly Hills. Her passenger is Victoria (Gena Rowlands), a power-tongued casting agent who wields her cellular phone like an Uzi. The finely calibrated teamwork of Ryder and Rowlands suggests there's more at stake than a fare.

In the cocoon of the cab, the two women trade war stories. Though a generation separates them, Victoria sees star potential in the foulmouthed driver. Corky, maybe the only one in greater Los Angeles who doesn't want to make it in the movies, would rather be a mechanic. The conflict drives a wedge between them.

Admirers of the director's minimalist, deadpan style in *Stranger Than Paradise, Down by Law* and *Mystery Train* may be thrown by such Jarmusch firsts as big stars, a fat (for him) budget and a grand canvas. But the joke is that Jarmusch has traveled all over the globe and put his actors on wheels only to create a still life. Abetted by the haunted bleat of Tom Waits's vocals and the spare elegance of Frederick Elmes's cinematography, Jarmusch makes the world whizzing by those taxi windows a thing of beauty and terror, but if caught only in glimpses. More than ever, Jarmusch bypasses traditional narrative in favor of mood and stasis.

The film's formal structure emerges more clearly in the second story. In New York, Helmut (Armin Mueller-Stahl), an East German who can barely drive, picks up Yo-Yo (Giancarlo Esposito), a black Brooklynite who needs a cab home. On the way they collect Angela (Rosie Perez), Yo-Yo's outspoken sister-in-law. The culture clash is hilarious, letting Perez – the dynamo of *White Men Can't Jump* – add more luster to her rising star. But now there's an edge to the laughter.

By the time of the third story, set in Paris, the edge is cutting. A cabby from the Ivory Coast (Isaach De Bankolé) questions his beautiful and blind French passenger (a fiercely funny Béatrice Dalle) and learns some hard lessons about condescending to the handicapped.

The comedy gets wilder and blacker in the fourth story, as a Roman cabby (Roberto Benigni, the convict clown of *Down by Law)* improvises a confession to an old priest (Paolo Bonacelli) dozing in the back seat. Jarmusch has written a marvel of a monologue for Benigni, whose comic dexterity makes it a tour de force.

In the last story, set in Helsinki, the sorrow that tinges the humor in the other tales runs deep. The driver (Matti

> {EVEN BEFORE I MET JIM, I KNEW HE HAD TO BE VERY SENSITIVE, BECAUSE HIS MOVIES HAVE SO MUCH HUMANITY AND KINDNESS IN THEM. BUT WORKING WITH HIM VERIFIED IT.}

Pellonpää) and his three drunken passengers (Kari Väänänen, Sakari Kuosmanen and Tomi Salmela) try to laugh off their problems with jobs and families. But when despair overcomes one man left at the curb side at dawn, Jarmusch's gift for locating the poetry in displacement is movingly realized.

It's possible to criticize *Night on Earth* on a story-by-story basis as fast or dull or sad. It's possible but irrelevant, since the film's cumulative power is what matters, and that power is undeniable. Director Jim Jarmusch is a true visionary; he knows his films can't bring order to the ravishing chaos around him, but he can't resist the fun of trying. In this compassionate comedy of missed connections, he makes us see the ordinary in fresh and pertinent ways. But the flickers of humanity in those taxis are soon dulled by barriers of time, sex, race, language and money. They are flickers in a vast emotional void. In Jarmusch's decidedly un-Disneyish view, it's not a small world after all.
~ *By Peter Travers*

Bram Stoker's

DRACULA

{ BY THE DIRECTOR & CAST
US, *November 1992* }

AS A TEENAGER, I WORKED AS THE drama counselor at a camp. One summer, I read *Dracula* to my group of eight- and nine-year-old boys. When we got to that chilling moment – when Harker looks out the window and sees Dracula crawling across the face of the wall like a bug – even those little boys knew, this was going to be good! I was about fourteen when I saw the Bela Lugosi film. I loved him, but I was disappointed by the three vampire brides – they were just standing there in their robes, looking dead, and that wasn't what a fourteen-year-old boy wants to see. ★ I remember as a kid going to the *Encyclopedia Britannica* to look up Dracula and there he was, Vlad the Impaler. I was just thrilled to think he really existed. In his script, Jim Hart uses the history of Prince Vlad to set the frame for the whole story. It's full of passion and eroticism. The brides aren't just

LEFT: ON THE SET OF 'BRAM STOKER'S DRACULA' RYDER SIDLES UP WITH HER DIRECTOR FRANCIS FORD COPPOLA, 1992

standing around; they actually rape Harker – when I read it, it filled my child's heart with enthusiasm.

Dracula's been portrayed as a monster or as a seducer, but knowing his biography made me think of him as a fallen angel, as Satan. The irony is that he was this hero who single-handedly stopped the Turks, but then he renounced God because his wife was a suicide and was denied holy burial. Usually Dracula is just a reptilian creature in a horror film. I wanted people to see that underneath this vampire myth is really fundamental human stuff that everyone feels and knows.

Blood is the primary metaphor. Even if people don't feel a sacramental relationship with God, I think they can understand how many people renounce their blood ties to the creative spirit or whatever it is – and become

W I N O N A

RYDER 79

like the living dead. The vampire has lost his soul, and that can happen to anyone."

{GARY OLDMAN} "Playing Dracula was a nice tradition to step into. One of the joys of playing him is that there's a good side and a bad side to him that run parallel with one another. In the movie he is shown in many forms. I liked the old man the best, partly because you only see that character in Transylvania, where nothing can harm him. In those scenes I invested him with a lot of wit and humor. I had him play with Harker rather like a cat would play with a mouse. Dracula's only vulnerable when he becomes young and goes to London, because he's found his love again. He's in love, and he's vulnerable – like all of us. He gets fucked up over a chick. Love will get you every time. I also play a green mist in the film. But it's a secret how I turn my body into that. I hung out with a smoke machine for a long time to pick up the technique. I don't think even Brando did that. As Dracula, I'm playing someone who's undead. I'm playing the [living dead]. How did I get into that? I did some research: I spent some time in Hollywood."

{KEANU REEVES} "I play Jonathan Harker, who Francis has described as a yuppie. I just had so much fun doing this movie. The cast is amazing . . . amazing! I got to act with Gary Oldman, Winona Ryder, Anthony Hopkins. Anthony is a beautiful man and an amazing actor. Working with him was a lesson in life and also in acting. He's got monster craft. There's one scene in the movie where I'm pinned down by these vampire brides. A lot of people would say to me, 'Hey dude, you're lucky.' But these women are carnivores. When Harker enters that room, he sort of goes under a trance. When Dracula comes in, the spell is broken, and the horror and the insanity and the gruesome evil dawn on him. He's revolted and goes into extreme shock. I mean, he goes mad. He's seen the devil. And these are the witches from the pit of hell. We took a lot of days to shoot that scene. By the end it was great because we just got *more blood!* And we did *crazy things!* Francis was *spinning* the

camera and we were *biting* and *screaming* and *pulling* and *biting!* That was a lot of fun."

{WINONA RYDER} "When I was sent the script for *Dracula*, I thought it was just fascinating and really beautifully written, with lines that I still sometimes mutter because they're so wonderful. My character, Mina, is way ahead of her time. She's very independent, but at the same time she's struggling with wanting to be a good, dutiful wife [to Harker]. In those days, people were so restricted by the clothing and the manners. Then this man, Dracula, comes and he releases all of that, and you feel this wild sense of abandonment. You see the darker side of yourself. It's like . . . I don't want to say a fantasy, because that makes it sound like people would want that. It's just very ethereal and mythical and mystical."

{ANTHONY HOPKINS} "I played Van Helsing as a strange, maverick medicine man. A quack doctor-cum-genius. Before I took the part, I didn't really know who Van Helsing was. I started reading the book about two years ago, but I thought, God, this is heavy going. I didn't really enjoy it. So I left it. We had a good time filming the movie. I felt like Dad on the film. I would do my Hannibal Lecter for Winona; she enjoyed that. But mostly I would stay in my trailer and read my books, then I'd go out on the set and never know what to expect because it was like going into a great cauldron. Francis is like a great chef; he puts in all these ingredients and cooks this huge pasta."

{SADIE FROST} "Lucy is precocious, young and beautiful. Then Dracula just comes in and takes over. When Lucy dies she comes back as a vampire. She [sucks the blood] from young boys because she doesn't have the strength to attack a grown man. That was a very upsetting scene for me to shoot because I had to carry a baby – who was absolutely terrified of me – down these stairs with this huge dress on. I was very upset that day. I didn't want to be a nightmare in this child's mind for the rest of her life, which I'm probably going to be. The scene in my tomb where Cary Elwes, who plays my fiancé, puts the stake in my heart was also pretty scary. In rehearsal I would never plan to scream, but I did every time." W

PRECEDING PAGES: RYDER IN HER MINA HARKER COSTUME; RIGHT: RYDER WITH GARY OLDMAN DRESSED AS COUNT DRACULA

US, *September 1993*

Martin Scorsese's
PERIOD PIECE
{By Lawrence Frascella}

"BEAUTY COMBINED WITH BRUTALITY" is how director Martin Scorsese characterizes his new film, *The Age of Innocence.* Depending on your definition of beauty, those words could describe any Scorsese movie – from the magnificent *Raging Bull* to the maximal *Cape Fear.* Still, a costume drama based on a 1920 novel by Edith Wharton represents a major shift for the master of urban violence and whacked virility. And that's exactly what makes *The Age of Innocence* the most eagerly anticipated movie of the fall.

The film stars Daniel Day-Lewis as Newland Archer, the scion of an aristocratic New York family (circa late 1800s) who falls in love with the married Countess Olenska (Michelle Pfeiffer) on the eve of his engagement to the socially inviolable May Welland (Winona Ryder). On the surface, this well-mannered story seems straight out of the Merchant-Ivory school of ever-so-proper filmmaking. But when Scorsese starts talking about flashing images that look like "streaks of paint" and a ballroom scene made up of four long, risky, unbroken takes, you know you've ventured far from the stodgy charms of *Masterpiece Theatre.*

But how did Scorsese wind up on Wharton's turf in the first place? In 1980, he was given the book by a friend, screenwriter and journalist Jay Cocks, who simply said, "This one is you." He had to read it several times before the story clicked. A closer look revealed themes that are very New York and very Catholic and, therefore, very Scorsese. "I've always been attracted to the repression of desire," he explains. "The love that's not consummated, the love that becomes an obsession, that theme has gone through many of my movies. It goes back to *Taxi Driver.*

"At one point, Daniel Day-Lewis's character goes to find Michelle at a country home and he sees her parasol. He puts it to his mouth and nose and takes in its scent. I'm interested in that sort of thing, the way he looks at the shape of her neck while she's seated at a table. It's obsessive. He's overwhelmed."

Even with a director of Scorsese's stature at the helm, it's easier to get a green light for a thrill ride like *Cape Fear* than a seventy-five-year-old love story. The project originated at Twentieth Century Fox and passed through Universal before it landed at Columbia, where studio chief Mark Canton gave Scorsese plenty of time for post-production (filming wrapped back in June 1992) but a smaller budget than first anticipated. According to producer Barbara DeFina, the film cost less than $35 million, a surprisingly conservative figure considering the thousands of exquisite costumes, sumptuous production design and the dedication to period accuracy.

"The authenticity is almost another character," says DeFina. "We had experts who either studied the time or knew about it through family background. People spoke and acted so differently back then. Something as simple as walking out a door became a big deal. Marty's assistant director was responsible for a lot of that secondary action. By the end of the movie, he was able to give a formal dinner party for one hundred."

"The corsets were cinched in so tight," recalls Winona Ryder, "that when you had any sort of motion and you needed air, you felt very dizzy. My engagement ring alone must have been worth hundreds of thousands of dollars. It was very insured."

If Scorsese's insistence on all-around veracity seems admirable, he did not pursue it simply for visual effect. It is absolutely essential to the dramatic tone of the film. "These people may have held in their emotions," he says, "but their passion makes itself evident in the way they dress, the food, the decor. These details are what keep Newland Archer in place."

While filming *The Age of Innocence,* Michelle Pfeiffer told the press that Scorsese called it his most violent film. When asked to back up this claim, Scorsese laughs and says, "That was just a way of being provocative." But, he admits, "there is violence in it." To illustrate, he points to the American movie that most influenced his approach – the Montgomery Clift–Olivia de Havilland classic *The Heiress* (based on an 1881 novel by Henry James).

"I found it fascinating when the father, played by Ralph Richardson, explains to his daughter that Montgomery Clift is only interested in her money because, after all, she was quite plain. I was only eight or nine, and I was coming from a totally different working-class background, but I saw that, no matter how well they were dressed or properly they behaved, that was an absolutely devastating thing to tell his daughter. She never forgave him – and I've never forgotten it. If we've gotten any of *that* kind of drama, that would be great." ◼

W
I
N
O
N
A

THE AGE OF innocence

Rolling Stone, *September 30, 1993*

IN THIS CLASSIC LOVE STORY, Martin Scorsese sweeps us away on waves of dizzying eroticism and rapturous romance. Without bloodshed or a holler of "fuck you," Scorsese – the raging bull of directors – bursts into the china shop that is Edith Wharton's 1920 novel, *The Age of Innocence.* He roughs things up a bit, though nothing gets shattered except our preconceptions. Set in the posh watering holes of New York society in the 1870s, this thrillingly directed and acted drama deals with delicate matters far removed from the violent action of Scorsese's work from *Mean Streets* to *GoodFellas.* But look closer. Though a century apart, Scorsese and Wharton are both experts in New York's tribal warfare. Behind the elegant facade of Wharton's characters is a calculated cruelty that Scorsese's hoods could easily recognize.

Society is determined to wipe out the budding relationship between lawyer Newland Archer (Daniel Day-Lewis) and Countess Ellen Olenska (Michelle Pfeiffer), the married cousin of May Welland (Winona Ryder), to whom Archer is engaged. Archer and his fiancée represent two of the finest families in New York. They belong. The countess does not. Though she's a granddaughter of the formidably fat but kindly Mrs. Mingott (the superb Miriam Margolyes), Olenska has married a foreigner – like her mother before her – and lived in scandalous European circles. It's the count's infidelities that send Olenska home to seek a divorce. Society is sympathetic to her plight but not to what it perceives as her boldness in speech and dress and her seduction of Archer.

Organized crime could take lessons in closing ranks from these reigning families, celebrated by the social arbiters

Sillerton Jackson (Alec McCowen) and Larry Lefferts (Richard E. Grant). The countess must be forced back to Europe and her relationship with Archer destroyed and all this accomplished without the slightest indication that behind the polite courtesies lies a brutal conspiracy carried out with the formality of an execution.

Spurning *Masterpiece Theatre* twittiness, Scorsese cuts to the primal passions of Wharton's tale. He and cowriter Jay Cocks, a former film critic for *Time,* find a kinship with Wharton in the urge to challenge rules that crush the rebel spirit. Wharton grew up under the iron glove of New York aristocracy and escaped it by settling in Europe. She was fifty-eight when *The Age of Innocence* was published. The novel was a backward glance to a time when she identified strongly with the limited choices facing Archer and the countess.

A superlative cast catches Wharton's urgency. Ryder, at her loveliest, finds the guile in the girlish May – she'll use any ruse that will help her hold on to Archer. Day-Lewis is smashing as the man caught between his emotions and the social ethic. Not since Olivier in *Wuthering Heights* has an actor matched piercing intelligence with such imposing good looks and physical grace. Pfeiffer gives the performance of a lifetime with her brilliantly nuanced portrayal of the outcast countess. With her hair in tight curls that accentuate her pale beauty, she seems lit from within.

For a movie about two people who never consummate their desire, *Age* is alive with sensuality that draws inspiration from sources as diverse as Luchino Visconti's *Senso* and William Wyler's *The Heiress.* The lovers must struggle to steal a few moments alone. Scorsese makes repression seem wantonly erotic as Archer caresses the folds of the countess's gown, presses his lips to the tip of her parasol. Archer is intoxicated with this woman, whose beauty and frank wit shatter his inherited ideas about respectability. "Each time I see you," he says, "you happen to me all over again."

No screen couple has ever been this sexy with their clothes on. Scorsese stages their most touching scene in a horse-drawn carriage, huddled together against the forces that divide them. The costumes of Gabriella Pescucci, however sumptuous, erect another barrier. Even the countess's gloves have buttons. When Archer manages to expose the flesh of her wrists and rub it against his cheek, the moment packs genuine carnal sizzle. Startled in midkiss by the flash of a street lamp through the carriage window, Archer foresees a place where the two can be together without hiding. The countess is less naive. "Oh, my dear – where is that country?" she asks.

While Scorsese and Cocks deserve credit for staying faithful to Wharton, they err in trying to include too much of her voice. Joanne Woodward narrates with tart elegance, speaking passages directly from the novel. It works in the early ballroom scene, when the denizens of society are introduced in a witty parody of *GoodFellas.* Instead of being introduced to Freddy Nonose, Pete the Killer and

RYDER (WHO PLAYED MAY WELLAND) AND MICHELLE PFEIFFER (HER RIVAL COUNTESS ELLEN OLENSKA) FLANK 'AGE OF INNOCENCE' DIRECTOR MARTIN SCORSESE AT THE FILM'S PREMIERE, 1993

Frankie the Wop, we're meeting the ultrasnooty Van der Luydens, Henry (Michael Gough) and Louisa (the late Alexis Smith), and the nouveau riche Beauforts, Julius (Stuart Wilson) and Regina (Mary Beth Hurt).

It works less well when the narrator tells us what to think. The device is most damaging when Archer and May give their first dinner party as young marrieds in honor of the countess's departure for Europe. The scene itself is superb, with the actors showing the pain each character is feeling behind their idle chatter. Then comes that voice: "From the seamless performance of this ritual, Archer knew that New York believed him to be Madame Olenska's lover. And he

understood for the first time that his wife shared that belief." The voice-over steps on what the actors are doing and distracts us from making our own judgments.

That the heavy narration doesn't crush the film is a tribute to the artistry of one of the best directors in the world. *The Age of Innocence* is a visual feast in which Scorsese and his collaborators – cinematographer Michael Ballhaus and editor Thelma Schoonmaker – ravish the senses. Take the opening scene at the opera house. It starts on close-ups of small details – the singer's painted mouth, the gardenia in Archer's lapel, the blur of jewels and clothes seen through opera glasses. Then the full view as the countess extends her fan across the expanse of

the theater, and we catch our breath in amazement.

But beneath the dazzle, Scorsese finds the details that define character. At the end of the film, a much older Archer sits on a bench outside the countess's Paris apartment. He ignores pleas from his grown son (Robert Sean Leonard) to call on the woman who almost snatched him from the jaws of conformity. The past is frozen in Archer's memory, along with his feelings. Seven decades after its debut, *The Age of Innocence* touches a nerve that owes nothing to cozy nostalgia. Scorsese has made the most extravagantly heartfelt film of his career about the impossibility of believing that love conquers all.   *~ Peter Travers*

I THINK WINONA'S THE POSTER GIRL OF EVERY TREKKIE EVERY COMPUTER NERD, EVERY COMEDY HEAD AND EVERY COMIC BOOK COLLECTOR. } JANEANE GAROFALO AND ATHLETES, TOO. YOU KNOW? SHE'S SO GORGEOUS THAT SHE CROSSES OVER

WINONA

She's No "Midget Freak"

Rolling Stone, *March 10, 1994*

{By Jeff Giles}

WINONA RYDER thinks reading me her diaries is a dreadful idea. I beg her in the name of science, medicine and anything else I can think of. We talk it over. And over. I tell her she would be giving a gift to the readers – something pure, unfiltered, straight from the mountain spring. She tells me that hauling out those spiral notebooks would be "the cheesiest, tackiest thing in the world." Still, she mulls it over. For weeks, she says neither yes nor no. Instead, I get the message you occasionally get from those old Magic 8 Balls: REPLY HAZY, TRY AGAIN.

On New Year's Day, Ryder calls from her place in New York, and this time the Magic 8 Ball says, incredibly, SIGNS POINT TO YES. The twenty-two-year-old actress lives in a gorgeous, stately apartment building in Manhattan – an ocean liner drifting through a gray and dingy neighborhood. Tonight, Ryder's friend Kevin Haley and her boyfriend, Dave Pirner of Soul Asylum, are downstairs cooking dinner. The actress is in her bedroom, sipping tea with honey. She's a friend among friends, a homebody at home. And there's a stack of diaries on her bed. "I can hardly read my writing," she says. But she does. Ryder reads an entry, from April Fools' Day 1993, which she wrote while in Portugal, shooting Bille August's muddled epic *The House of the Spirits.* At the time, she was tumbling toward the end of long-standing relationships with insomnia (five years) and Johnny Depp (four). So the first entry is as follows: "Lisbon. Yikes. Weirdness." And we're off.

"I can't believe I did that," Ryder says, laughing, fifteen minutes later. "I can't believe I read you my journals. That's so lame. Oh, God. Are you totally going to have a heyday with me? Are you going to *crush* me?"

LIVE AND IN PERSON, Ryder is five feet four inches and weighs one hundred and three pounds. In a corset, her waist measures seventeen inches. Joanne Gardner, media coordinator for the Polly Klaas Foundation, calls Ryder "teeny-tiny." Martin Scorsese, who directed Ryder's revelatory turn in *The Age of Innocence,* refers to her as a "person of *that* stature." Janeane Garofalo, who plays her roommate in Ben Stiller's dead-on Generation X comedy *Reality Bites,* puts it this way: "She's so small! I mean, she's like a little figurine for the coffee table!"

Upon acquaintance, Ryder will charm you within an inch of your life. She'll be geeky ("I don't think I'd be good at trashing dressing rooms. I'd be like 'Ouch!' "), censorious ("I can't *believe* you liked that movie. I'm surprised, and I'm disappointed. I really am. I'm not kidding"), indignant ("They offered me that movie, by the way, and I wrote a very nasty letter saying, 'How *dare* you?' "), then geeky once more ("I never sent it"). Still, your first impression of Ryder is simply that she is lovely and small. With her knees drawn up to her chest and her head hung low, she is a ball that could roll away at any minute. Ryder's size clearly makes her feel vulnerable – outdoors, she walks with a hunched, defensive posture – but often she makes light of it. One afternoon, walking barefoot through the vast, chandeliered lobby of her apartment building, she turns and says: "All the famous models live here. I feel like a midget fuckin' freak."

NTERVIEW NUMBER ONE falls on a blank, gray day shortly before Christmas. Ryder has just returned from the memorial service for Polly Klaas, the twelve-year-old girl who was abducted last October in the actress's hometown, Petaluma, California, and found murdered two months later. Ryder arrives at the restaurant precisely on time and kisses Pirner goodbye in the street. (Later, I'll ask if I can meet with him, and the Magic 8 Ball will deliberate for weeks.) Once inside, she sits in a corner and removes her "Holden Caulfield hat": a plaid hunting cap with fur-lined earflaps. Her hair is startlingly short. "My mom cut my hair off," she says. "It wasn't my natural color, and she was like 'Oh, honey, *let* me.' Now my ears are always freezing." She gestures at her hat. "So I need earflaps."

Ryder seems relaxed and settled in, but the moment I turn on the tape recorder, she stares at it as if looking into oncoming headlights. Anyone about to be subjected to weeks' worth of questions is entitled to a case of the jitters – Truman Capote referred to the movie star and the reporter as "the nervous hummingbird and its would-be captor." And for a while, Ryder gets smaller and smaller, threatening to vanish. "I get nervous," she says, "and when I get nervous, I get inarticulate." She orders herbal tea and chicken soup. I ask if she remembers the first time she had insomnia. She looks at the tape recorder again, then takes the leap.

"I was in Memphis doing *Great Balls of Fire!*," she says. "I was sixteen. I was sick, so I was kind of delirious, and I remember doing the weirdest thing. I took a bunch of grapefruits. . . . You know when you're sick, and you have a fever? And you pick up an orange or a grapefruit, and they're comforting because they're cold, so you put them on your face? [X singer] John Doe was playing my dad in the movie, and he brought over a bunch of grapefruits. For vitamin C and stuff. So I put the grapefruits all over, like surrounding me in the bed. And I just laid there and tried to sleep." Was this Doe's idea?

Ryder laughs. "No, no, no. It was my idea. I mean, you get bored. I remember just panicking. And the digital clock was going: 3:30! 4:30! 5:30! I stayed up the whole night. I remember – as it got light – it was just the saddest thing to me. I thought I was going to die or something. And from that night on . . . because I knew it could happen, it did happen."

Weeks later, I remind Ryder of the tale of the grapefruit. "Oh, God," she groans. "*Why* did I tell you that story? *What* was my point? Hey, maybe the grapefruits gave me insomnia for five years."

OVER THE NEXT COUPLE OF WEEKS, Ryder will occasionally retreat into her nervous-hummingbird routine. This will take some explaining. With *Heathers,* which she narrated via her character's journals, Ryder entered her generation's circulatory system. Teenage life was twisted, and Ryder, more than any other actor or actress, was in on the joke. Since *Heathers,* movies

like *The Age of Innocence* – and even Francis Ford Coppola's overripe *Bram Stoker's Dracula* – have made Ryder something more than the doyenne of Generation X. They've made her a movie star. Stiller says: "It's funny – girls really like her, and guys really like her. Every guy I've ever talked to has a crush on her." Garofalo says, "I've noticed that even little, little kids like her," adding, "I think Winona's the poster girl of every Trekkie, every computer nerd, every comedy head and every comic-book collector. And athletes, too. You know? She's so gorgeous that she crosses over."

Ryder has already won the Golden Globe for Best Supporting Actress for *The Age of Innocence,* and this March she could win the Oscar ("Oh, shut up!"). Rumor has it that she's being offered as much as $4 million a picture. The actress loves a period piece: In *The House of the Spirits,* a political saga spanning four generations, she plays the defiant daughter of a conservative Latin American statesman (Jeremy Irons), and soon she'll begin work on a new adaptation of one of Polly Klaas's favorite books, *Little Women.* But Ryder's not ditching her core audience: In the wickedly satiric *Reality Bites,* she plays a young, unemployable filmmaker whose young, unemployable love interest (Ethan Hawke) threatens to turn her apartment into "a den of slack." Says Ryder, "My agent said, 'I think you're going to like this movie, because you can wear jeans in it.' "

THE ONE THING Ryder seems not to have learned on the way to becoming a movie star is how to lie. Hence the nervous hummingbird. She thinks things through. Is she being honest? Is she being fair? Is she being defensive or tacky? If insomnia didn't exist, Ryder would have invented it. One night, she calls with a small hard sound in her voice and blurts, apropos of her diaries, "If you're only pretending to like me, and you write a really mean article, I'm going to *hate* myself for giving you fuel." I stammer assurances. Ryder wants to know how I'll use the diaries. I tell her I'll just stick them in somewhere. Now she's laughing – "What, in the middle of the article?"

{APRIL 8, 1981}

I wish I could write in this fucking thing without the fear of it being read or fucking published one day. Hell, I'm not that famous. Who the fuck cares anyway? I'll probably be dead by then, so it won't really matter. Unless my kids find this shit embarrassing. . . .

I wish I were in San Francisco, in the Sunset district. I remember going there once with G. I got so much sand in my shoes. He had a skateboard, and we were walking on the beach. I felt so much older than him, but part of me didn't. . . . Boy, did I blow him off. I remember he was so poor, as poor as I used to be. He was so dirty. He was so sweet. I didn't like him, though – not like that. Maybe for a minute, but it went away. . . . Right now I wish I had a little apartment in San Francisco. I wish I wasn't doing what I was doing. No, that's wrong. I like what I'm doing – I just don't like part of it. Classic, huh? This sounds so classic: actors bitching and moaning about wanting to be like everybody else. But if they were, they'd just want to be movie stars. I can live how I want. That's that. No one put this wall up. No one else knelt down around me and laid the bricks. I did it myself. That's why I'm so exhausted. Or is it jet lag?

I love this line in Tom Waits' "San Diego Serenade": "Never felt my heart strings until I went insane." I'm having a beer. Oh, fucking boy! Isn't that exciting? It actually is, if you think about it. For me, at least. These are things I never do because I think too much. I think ahead. I think behind. I think sideways. I think it all. If it exists, I've fucking thought of it.

RYDER WROTE THAT THREE YEARS ago on a plane from London to Los Angeles. She'd had half a beer and was already tipsy. Ryder is the product of a bohemian, countercultural childhood, although strangely so. Her parents once wrote a scholarly, feminist book called *Shaman Woman, Mainline Lady,* which identified them as the directors of "the only library in the world exclusively devoted to literature of mind-altering drugs." Ryder once wrote a journal entry in which she joked about her "fear of marijuana." Her parents took the kids to splash around naked in waterfalls. Ryder now says of nudity in movies: "I just couldn't do it. I just couldn't. No matter what. I just couldn't."

Today, Ryder's father deals in Sixties-related books, and her mother has a tiny production company that specializes in the filming of births. The actress frequently reminisces about Petaluma – the sentence *I miss my family* is murmured like a mantra through her journals. Ryder has a half sister, Sunyata, twenty-five, and a half brother, Jubal, twenty-four, from her mother's previous marriage, as well as a younger brother, Yuri, seventeen, who is named after the first Russian in space. In her stories the clan seems sweet, funny, infinitely gentle. Grapefruit clearly didn't give Ryder insomnia. More likely, it had to do with spending her adolescence on sets and in hotel rooms. It had to do with pining for Petaluma and with trying to think sideways.

"For a long time, I was almost ashamed of being an actress," Ryder says. "I felt like it was a shallow occupation. I'd go see a band with friends from school, and people would be watching every move I made. They'd be judging me: 'Look at her shoes! I bet those cost four hundred dollars!' That affected me. I grew up with no money. My parents did what they were passionate about, and they didn't make money. And there were a lot of kids, so we lived with no electricity, no running water and no heating, except for a stove. Every week my dad would get a pint of Häagen-Dazs, and that was our big exciting reward. My parents compensated with amazing amounts of love and support, so I don't regret any of it. But my point is that when people look at me like I'm this really rich, pampered, privileged person – I am. I am right now. But it wasn't always like that. Sometimes people think I was born on the screen and that I kind of walked into the world. Sometimes I'll meet people, and they'll be like 'Oh, I'm *really* sorry about my car. It's *really* dirty.' I mean, we had moss and mushrooms growing in our car. If we *had* a car."

Ryder often beats me to the next question. "Why am I so defensive? I'm defensive because it offends me so much when

. . . Okay, I don't want to fuck this up. . . . I know a lot of young actors who live in these *dumps.* They have their books scattered, and their mattress is on the floor – and they're *millionaires.* That's fine. That's their way of living. But the reason they're doing it is that they're ashamed. And I've talked to them about it. You just want to say, 'Don't live this way to show people that you're *real* and that you're *deep.*' It offends me, because I know what it's like to be in poverty, and it's not fun, and it's not romantic, and it's not *cool.*"

Last year, Ryder wrote in her diary: "I feel like it's OK to be who I am. It's OK to be a fucking movie star. It's OK to live in a nice house."

RYDER LIVES IN A NICE HOUSE. And she can sleep – in a bed, on a plane, anywhere. One Sunday, I'm sitting in her lobby, waiting for her to make it out of bed. Soon she comes whispering down the hall. In a striped shirt and overalls, she has the warm, disheveled look of someone who has just woken up and isn't quite sure where she is. She apologizes for running late. She says to the concierge, "Any mail?" The concierge says: "No, Miss Ryder. No mail on Sundays." And she laughs at herself: "I forgot it was Sunday."

Back in her apartment, Ryder gives me a shy, offhand tour. Hers is a spare, modern place: high white ceilings, lots of light. In the living room there's a grand piano and an acoustic guitar leaning against a couch. And there's an ink stain in the middle of the beige carpet: Last night, Pirner was writing Christmas cards. (I've again asked to meet the singer but may have blown it by saying, "What's up with his hair?" To which Ryder replied: "Aww. His hair is *fine.* He just hasn't brushed it in ten years.") Elsewhere: an issue of the *Missing Children Report* and a photo album from *The Age of Innocence,* in which Scorsese has written, "To Winona: You 'became' May Welland by incorporating all the delight, beauty and strength that you already possess." Ryder is just settling into this apartment. Her first editions (Jane Austen, E.M. Forster) and original letters (Albert Einstein, Oscar Wilde) are back in Los Angeles. Separated from her worldly possessions, she seems frustrated: "I wish I had more things that *reveal character.*"

Here's the thing about Ryder – she reveals her character in stages. It's no coincidence that she played the hell out of Welland, who begins *The Age of Innocence* as a giddy bride-to-be and ends it as a shrewd, willful wife. After leaving her apartment, Ryder and I browse for an hour and a half in Tower Books – she agrees to leave only when I promise we'll go to another bookstore later – then settle in at a bright, clinking coffee shop. The actress is in top form: funny, feisty, unafraid of the tape recorder. I would like to discuss the foolish, oversexed *Dracula,* but when I broached the subject during an earlier interview, the hummingbird and I had the following exchange:

Q: Let's talk about *Dracula.*
A: Okay, I felt really connected to *Age of Innocence* because . . .
Q: Wait, I'm not letting you off the hook that easily.
A: I don't know what to say about it that's . . .

Q: Let's talk about its amazing similarity to the new Meat Loaf video. Have you seen that?

A: Yeah. [*Extremely nervous laugh*] Yeah.

Here's what I mean about Ryder revealing herself in stages. Today, I remind her of a *Premiere* article about the making of *Dracula*. The story opened with Coppola goading Ryder through a scene by shouting from off camera, "You *whore! You fucking whore!*" The writer of the article described this as "just the push Ryder needs." I ask her if it was.

Ryder cranks up the sarcasm: "Oh, yeah, it was really great. I love being called a bitch and a whore. It's a completely silly technique, and it does not work." She pauses. "I would never have bad-mouthed *Dracula* at the time. Luckily, now I don't need to be Francis Coppola's favorite actress to have a good career. Now I know I can have my opinion and still be respected. But before, I was scared, because he was just so intimidating. I thought if I spoke out, people would think I was insane."

TWO THINGS HAVE GIVEN RYDER the courage of her convictions and finally made her realize it's okay to be a "fucking movie star." The first, very simply, was *The Age of Innocence*. *Heathers* is Ryder's best friend, but *Age* is the man she wants to marry. "It was the first time I ever felt proud of myself as an actress," she says. "And it really made it hard for me because *nothing* compares." Says Scorsese: "I think she's reacting to being part of a labor of love. We had a very good time. Winona has a good sense of humor, and her energy is boundless. It was like having *rampant youth* on the set. She'd be jumping up and down, but then when you said, 'Action,' she froze into position. All that energy was put behind her eyes, and I found that really fascinating."

Ryder's second rite of passage was more complicated and far darker: It was the search for Klaas. The actress holed up with Klaas's family, helped scour the fields and man the hot line. And according to Polly's father, Marc, "She single-handedly put the story back on the front pages" by offering a $200,000 reward. "To me, it really wasn't a *cause,*" says Ryder, now on the Klaas Foundation's board of directors. "It was like 'This is an outrage, and it's outrageous that more people aren't outraged.' When something happens to a child, the world should stand still." Ryder found a noble use for something she'd previously been ashamed of: "my celebrityism, or whatever you call it." And she sorted through some of her own fears, past and present. After all, here is a woman not much bigger than a girl. A woman who has been stalked, though she has been advised not to discuss it. A woman who on New Year's Eve was grabbed by a drunk shouting, "Winona!" – an experience so unnerving that she returned to her great fortress of a home.

Ryder worries that people might dismiss her involvement in the Klaas case as a Hollywood photo op, but clearly it was no such thing. Joanne Gardner of the Klaas Foundation remembers the actress's first phone call: "She was in a hotel lobby in Los Angeles, sobbing. She said, 'This is my town. This is my junior high. What can I do? Do you need money?' We talked for an hour and a half. Winona had an awful lot of

experience, because she'd had some horrible experiences of her own – being stalked and all that. She had some psychologists that she knew. She had some FBI people that she knew. I mean, this woman . . . I've always been a fan, and she's a lovely little creature, but she astonished me with her grasp of the situation. This is not let's-go-open-a-shopping-mall kind of stuff. This is life-in-the-balance kind of stuff."

JUST AFTER NEW YEAR'S, Ryder and I are scheduled to have dinner, and she asks if I would mind eating at her place: She doesn't feel up to going out. I ask if anyone will be joining us, and against all odds, signs point to Pirner. This is the Magic 8 Ball's bravest hour – if you can't go to a bar without a drunk screaming your name, then whatever privacy you do have triples in value. Which reminds me of what Ryder says about Johnny Depp: not a hell of a lot. She never makes an unkind remark about him, on or off the record. Perhaps to aid in her never-ending quest to be gracious, she doesn't read Depp's press and hasn't seen *Benny and Joon* or *What's Eating Gilbert Grape.* I ask her to free-associate on WINONA FOREVER.

Q: Do you ever think about Johnny's tattoo?
A: No.
Q: When you were breaking up, did you think about the tattoo?
A: No.
Q: Well, now that you're thinking about the tattoo . . .
A: What do you want me to say? It's like 'It's there. Oh, well.' If I hated him, I'd probably say something mean. If I was still in love with him, I'd probably say something poignant. He's a great guy, but I really don't think about it.

That didn't yield much. I ask Ryder about the life of a celebrity couple, and she's more expansive: "I remember us desperately hating being hounded. It was horrible, and it certainly took its toll on our relationship. Everyday we heard that we were either cheating on each other or that we were broken up, when we weren't. It was like this constant mosquito buzzing around us. . . . Now, I feel like I have an identity, whereas before I was so used to people telling me who I was. I was *Winona!* I was *precocious!* I was *adorable!* I was *sexy!* These labels were being slapped on me, and I didn't have any life outside of it, except when I went back to Petaluma."

Ryder would like to protect her relationship with Pirner from the media, insofar as it's possible. She's deliberately low-key about what she refers to as, simply, "a nice thing that's evolving." "Our relationship is different than any one I've ever had," she says. "It's just more casual. It's more of a friendship, really." She pauses, fishing for words. "What I'm basically saying is that it's not full of *drama,* which is really nice."

Ryder met Pirner at Soul Asylum's *MTV Unplugged* concert last spring. Janeane Garofalo remembers her waxing poetic about her new boyfriend: "I told her I couldn't take it anymore. She definitely exceeded her Pirner limit." In person, the singer, like his girlfriend, charms most everyone. Says Garofalo: "I thought he was really funny and cute and sweet. I have a crush on him." Still, the couple has inspired some cynicism. Courtney Love, who's never at a loss for words,

blurted out to a crowd, "Kurt is leaving me for Winona." *Spin* gave Ryder its I'm With the Band award. A reporter for *Sassy* asked some alternative rockers if they would go out with her, explaining, "It's my theory that boys start bands so they can get famous enough to attract Winona Ryder." I ask the actress if any of this upsets her. She smiles and quotes her brother Yuri, who's fond of moaning, "*Aww, why can't we all just get along?*"

The truth about Ryder and Pirner: They share the cooking and they take turns washing the dishes. It's 9:00 p.m., and the three of us are dining on green salad, linguini in a marinara sauce and roasted chicken and potatoes. At first, Ryder and Pirner appear so different as to cancel each other out. She drinks root beer; he drinks red wine. She wants to know if she should cut the chicken; he says, "Oh, just tear a leg off." Then, of course, there's the fact that Ryder is drug free and Pirner was recently seen in *Rolling Stone* scarfing down mushrooms in his tour bus so as to foil the Canadian border patrol.

Still, Ryder and Pirner intersect at many points. Both are curious and well read (during dinner, he uses the word *cognitive* twice in five minutes). Both are unaccustomed to sleeping at night (Pirner is a confirmed night owl and admits to being useless during daylight hours). And both can think sideways (Pirner wrote a song called "Homesick," which Ryder quoted in her journal months before she met him). In person, they have a sweet and easy chemistry. When one of them talks, the other stops, looks and listens. When Ryder goes to the kitchen, she pauses to put her arms around her boyfriend's neck – like a headlock, only nicer.

Pirner seems in awe of Ryder's career but not particularly envious. "The other day I heard Winona on the phone telling somebody that she didn't get in this for the money," he says. "What an absurd thing to have to say when acting was all you wanted to do since you were thirteen. I mean, the only aspiration I ever had was to be in a punk-rock band." Pirner seems protective of Ryder. And he seems struck by how unspoiled she remains – even after years of people minding her business. Over dessert, I ask Ryder to describe her appeal as an actress. She laughs, turns to Pirner and says, "What's my appeal, Dave?" To which he has a ready reply: "Your appeal is that you don't know what your appeal is."

I leave around midnight. Ryder sees me to the door – outside on the streets of New York, she may walk defensively, but at home she glides like the puck in an air-hockey set. I remember something the actress read to me from her journal, something she wrote just before she parted ways with insomnia and other sorrows: "What do I feel right now? Fragile, a little confused, heartachey, a little tired." And I remember that after she read it, she said to me: "If you print any of this, will you be sure to say that this is old, that this isn't how I am right now? Because I've grown up a lot." Well, some things never change: Tonight, the actress won't get any sleep for hours and hours. Still, it won't be because she's fragile or confused. It'll be because she and her night-owl friend are hanging out: reading, watching videos, maybe goofing around on the guitar. It's a new year, and – for all the right reasons – Winona Ryder will be up all night. **W**

Slack Is BEAUTIFUL

{ By Mark Morrison }
US, *March 1994*

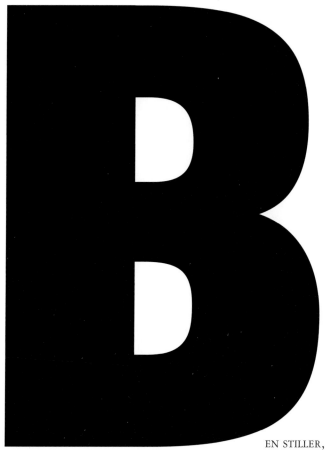

EN STILLER,
twenty-eight, is slumped in a back-row seat of a Hollywood screening room. The embodiment of Nineties cool in Stüssy wear and black work boots, he's putting his final stamp on *Reality Bites,* his feature-film directorial debut, in which he costars with Winona Ryder and Ethan Hawke. "I'd like that lighter," he says of one shot. "That's too dark," he says of another. Noticing that a character is momentarily obscured, he worries that the audience won't be able to see the actor's face. "Ben," chides his equally young cinematographer, Emmanuel "Chevo" Lubezki *(Like Water for Chocolate),* "you're getting too Hollywoodesque."

Best known for the glib pop-culture parodies (from Eddie Munster to Bruce Springsteen) that were the cornerstone of his Emmy-winning but ratings-losing 1992 Fox TV variety series, *The Ben Stiller Show,* Stiller may fear becoming too Hollywoodesque more than anything. With *Reality Bites,* he's determined to show he can create a commercial Hollywood movie without losing his edge. And this Nineties love story for the so-called twenty-nothings weaned on *Three's Company,* MTV and AIDS seems to be proving he can do just that.

{ SLACK MEETS SLICK }

Here's the pitch: Valedictorian Lelaina (Ryder) and her slacker best friend, Troy (Hawke), graduate from college in Houston and can't find jobs that in any way approach their abilities. She wants to make documentaries; he wants to make music. When she meets Michael (Stiller), a smoothie in a

Saab, her relationship with Troy is tested. Admittedly the plot doesn't sound like much. But generational movies seldom do – remember *Rebel Without a Cause? Bites* coproducer Michael Shamberg, also responsible for *The Big Chill,* says it was hard getting both pictures off the ground. "The studios didn't get it," he says. "Like *The Big Chill,* they didn't think *Reality Bites* was funny or had a story." Originally developed – then dropped – by TriStar, the movie was championed by younger agents at Creative Artists Agency, who attached hot clients Ryder and Hawke. Finally, Universal Studios came up with a modest $11.5 million budget.

To keep *Bites* from winding up a discourse on whiny white kids, the plot was streamlined into a love triangle set against a pop-culture panorama (look for cameos by MTV VJ Karen Duffy, the Lemonheads' Evan Dando, Soul Asylum's Dave Pirner and *The Firm*'s Jeanne Tripplehorn, Stiller's fiancée).

{ TRASH THE TRAILER PARK, HEAD FOR HOLLYWOOD }

A year ago, Helen Childress was holed up in a trailer park in Flagstaff, Arizona, when Winona Ryder called from Europe to heap praise on her *Reality Bites* script. Though flattered, the twenty-four-year-old first-time screenwriter doesn't claim to be the voice of her generation, just a member of it: "I have eight friends I thought were really funny at a time of my life I was very sentimental about."

It was at the University of Southern California, in 1990, that Childress wrote a screenplay that attracted Shamberg's attention. When she told him that most of her college friends were from broken homes (her parents divorced when she was thirteen) and that they faced limited job options – she had just been turned down for a job at Wendy's – he suggested she write her story.

Basing Lelaina loosely on herself, Childress modeled Troy on a classmate who is now her husband. And she peppered her script with cultural bytes from childhood. "I was a latch-key kid," she says. "I came home and turned on the TV. I can quote whole episodes of *The Brady Bunch* and *Good Times.*"

Twenty drafts later, Houston-born Childress says she's learned more about the film industry than she wants to know. "It was a great experience, but it made me realize that I just want to stay inside and write," she says.

Busily scripting another project for Ryder, Childress (who appears onscreen as a waitress) has yet to go to Hollywood. Her one Nineties-style splurge: "I bought a Nintendo."

{ IRONY RULES }

"Define irony." That's the line Ben Stiller gave his mother, Anne Meara, in a cameo as a prospective employer who rejects Ryder. Ben knows from irony – his parents are Sixties comedy duo Stiller and Meara. "What I have done in the comedy world is so different from my folks," he says. "But I feel this incredible pressure to be funny. In films, I don't want to do that."

Stiller's acting debut was at age ten on his mom's 1975 lawyer series, *Kate McShane.* Soon he was shooting Super 8 parodies in their Manhattan home. While appearing in a 1986 Lincoln Center production of *House of Blue Leaves* with Swoosie Kurtz and John Mahoney (who are featured in *Bites*), Stiller shot a parody of *The Color of Money* with Mahoney called *The Hustler of Money*. He sold it to *Saturday Night Live*. That led to a stint as a producer-host of a 1990 MTV sketch series and, subsequently, the Fox show.

In early 1992, Stiller joined *Reality Bites* as a director. As he and Childress retooled the script, he became the obvious choice to play Michael. And Stiller couldn't resist biting the hand that fed: His character is a workaholic executive at an MTV-like network called In Your Face. "The first meeting I ever had at MTV was with a middle-level executive," recalls Stiller. "I was saying, 'I have this idea for these three-minute segments.' He said, 'How about thirty seconds with crazy animation?' "

Stiller doesn't want life in his film reduced to reality bytes. "I learned a lot on this movie. For someone who did a lot of parody, I had to go for real emotion and risk doing something that could be made fun of."

{ SWEET INSPIRATIONS }

"I really wanted to wear jeans and lighten up a little bit," says Winona Ryder, when asked why she chose to play Lelaina.

After all, she spent the last several years – making the films *Bram Stoker's Dracula* and *The Age of Innocence* – trapped in period costumes. But what really attracted her to *Bites,* she says, was its core of optimism. "We don't give enough merit to sweetness in films," says the twenty-two-year-old actress. "Young actors are always trying to be so cool and dark – they want to go off and play serial killers."

Although *Reality Bites* is her most contemporary work since *Heathers,* Ryder found Lelaina more of an adjustment than it

> # MY AGENT SAID, "I THINK YOU'RE GOING TO LIKE 'reality BITES' BECAUSE YOU can wear jeans IN IT"
>
> Winona, *Rolling Stone, March 10, 1994*

might have been for a host of other young actresses. "I felt like a real outsider. . . . It seemed like everyone had gone through college and been broke. I couldn't relate to that. But I felt I understood it because my brother and sister and my best friend from Petaluma, where I grew up, are going through it now."

Unlike most of her peers, Ryder says her parents are still "madly in love." But she worries about her generation. "Something has gotten out of control. It seems crazy that people put so much stock in what's hip and what's not and don't appreciate the actual thing that it is."

This is Winona Ryder talking? The same one who was engaged to Johnny Depp and is now seeing Dave Pirner? Is this new awareness a reflection of her relationship with a rock star? "That's why it's been on my mind so much," she says.

{ STAND-UP GAL }

"I'm the alternative Eve Arden, man."

Maybe you've seen her on *The Ben Stiller Show* or *The Larry Sanders Show* or caught her stand-up routine on MTV. But as Ryder's hipster roommate Vickie, Janeane Garofalo, twenty-nine, joins the ranks of classic Hollywood scene-stealers.

At five foot one, Garofalo is shorter than Ryder but not exactly the fragile type. While Vickie is the one character in *Bites* whose parents aren't divorced, Garofalo's childhood was spent shuttling between her father in Houston and her mother in Madison, New Jersey.

She calls her performance in *Bites* "a testament to my lack of skill." But Ryder disagrees: "Janeane's incredibly brilliant. I thought she was the coolest person I ever met. She says the things I would think of a half hour after the fact."

It's this female bond that makes their scenes together fly. But it took a while to become chummy off screen. Says Ryder: "I gave her my number when we started rehearsing, and she didn't call me. A couple of weeks go by, and I go, 'How come you're not calling me?' And she's like: 'Are you serious? I'm way too freaked out to call you.' I said, 'But that's why I gave you my number.' She said, 'I thought you were just trying to be nice to me.' "

After shooting a pilot for HBO titled *Peep Show,* Garofalo will return to *Larry Sanders.* Despite industry buzz for her work in *Reality Bites,* she says: "I don't think it'll change my life. I don't think the Eve Ardens get that. So I'll have to be content with my lot in life as the rarely recognized actor."

{ COOL JERK THAWS OUT }

It happens in the "My Sharona" scene, when the old Knack tune starts blasting through the convenience store of a gas station, and Ryder, Garofalo and Steve Zahn, who plays their closeted gay friend, Sammy, begin dancing in the aisles. Ethan Hawke, all goatee and James Dean pout, just stands there clinging to his cool, the rock-star wanna-be with the 180 IQ who keeps a lid on every emotion. For Hawke, twenty-three, it's a breakthrough role after a decade of playing dull nice guys (the repressed schoolboy in *Dead Poets Society,* River Phoenix's pal in *Explorers,* Ted Danson's son in *Dad*).

"Troy is much more me," says Hawke, who spent his youth moving around with his mother after his parents divorced. After graduating from high school, he studied theater at Carnegie Mellon but dropped out to act full time. Today, he lives in New York City, where he is artistic director of a small theater company, Malaparte.

Like his contemporaries, Hawke shuns labels. "I don't think we're any more lost than anybody else was in this time period when you feel like you're not a kid but not a grown-up," he says. "This is a generation that will eventually have something to say. But I don't know why it's our job to say anything real clear right now." **W**

reaLITY BITeS

Rolling Stone, *March 10, 1994*

LIFE AFTER COLLEGE – the time between graduation and finding a job that pays your rent without making you puke. Panic time. By spinning something fresh out of something familiar, *Reality Bites* scores the first comedy knockout of the new year. It also brings out the vibrant best in Winona Ryder and Ethan Hawke as friends who resist being lovers, makes a star out of Janeane Garofalo as their tart-tongued buddy and puts Ben Stiller on the map as a director. The twenty-eight-year-old Stiller, who also acts in the film as a yuppie profiteer, pushes beyond the incisive parody of his late, lamented Fox TV series, *The Ben Stiller Show,* to reveal the fears that kick in after school's out. And debuting screenwriter Helen Childress, twenty-three, works playfully hip variations on the *Slacker-Singles* theme. Even when *Reality Bites* stoops to being glibly ingratiating, it gets the behavioral details right.

It's graduation day at an unnamed university in Texas. Class valedictorian Lelaina Pierce (Ryder) is trashing her parents' generation for trading in their Sixties ideals for a BMW and a pair of running shoes. Now that it's her turn to show up the sellouts, Lelaina is unnerved. She takes a four-hundred-dollar-a-week job as an assistant to a boobish local talk-show host (John Mahoney) who hates her "pointy little face" and intellectual condescension. Keep it "light and perky," he tells Lelaina. She thinks he's so cheesy she "can't watch him without crackers."

Still, the job helps pay the rent on the Houston apartment Lelaina shares with her best friend, Vickie (Garofalo), who's now a manager at the Gap and attending jeans-folding seminars. Is this what college prepared them for? Lelaina thinks not; she also thinks it's a bad idea to let another school chum, Troy (Hawke), move in. In Lelaina's view, Troy – an unemployed philosophy major slouching toward a career as a rock musician – will turn the apartment into a "den of slack." But Vickie persists. "He's strange, he's sloppy, he's a total nightmare for women," she admits. "I can't believe I haven't slept

with him yet." Garofalo, a regular on the Stiller series and HBO's acclaimed *Larry Sanders Show,* is a sensational comic find. She can lace a laugh with feeling in a unique way that promises a big future in movies.

Vickie lists the men she has slept with in a notebook; it was sixty-six at last count. Commitment scares her. As Lelaina says, "She's out the door before the condom comes off." It's Vickie and her friend Sammy (Steve Zahn), a closeted gay, who see the unspoken attraction that sparks the dis sessions between Lelaina and Troy. "Why don't you two just do it and get it over with," says Vickie. But Troy is more likely to cop an attitude than express emotion. Hawke (*Dead Poets Society, Alive!*) could have slid by on grunge sexiness. Instead, he finds reserves of passion in the hard case who doesn't want to end up like his working-stiff father, now dying of prostate cancer. "Hello," says Troy, answering the phone at home, "you've reached the winter of our discontent."

Reality Bites is that rare film that captures the strain unemployment puts on friendships as well as finances. "You eat and couch and fondle the remote control," Lelaina tells Troy in disgust. But when she's fired from the talk show, her behavior isn't much different. These characters take comfort in ducking reality through talking, toking, watching Seventies TV reruns and grooving to such oldie hits as Squeeze's "Tempted" and the Knack's "My Sharona." Lelaina captures all the fun and angst on her camcorder for a documentary she would like to sell to PBS. Instead, the footage winds up in the hands of Michael Grates (Stiller), an exec for the In Your Face cable channel ("It's like MTV but with an edge"). Michael falls hard for Lelaina and sees her videos as a perfect start for some reality programming. Stiller is wildly funny. He even makes us feel for this well-meaning college dropout who insists there's more to his life than a balance sheet. "I know why the caged bird sings," he says.

It's not likely. The jealous Troy hates Michael on sight ("he's the reason Cliffs Notes were invented") and laughs at Michael's inability to finish a coherent sentence. Angry over Troy's contempt, Michael snaps, "What's your glitch?" Hardly the *mot juste,* and Troy nails him for it. Michael may not have cool, but he has Lelaina. Or at least he does until she sees what a shallow package In Your Face makes of her reality videos, now cut down and tricked up with flashy graphics.

There are times when Stiller the director makes the same shambles of *Reality Bites.* The film's last half-hour degenerates into a cloyingly conventional romance that no amount of fancy editing, hit-soundtrack music and howlingly pretentious dialogue can disguise. "There's a planet of regret on my shoulders," Troy tells Lelaina in a drawn-out reconciliation scene that stops the movie and Hawke's performance cold. At these moments, *Reality Bites* is guilty of the very things it's criticizing.

But mostly the film shows a keen understanding of the anxiety that lies beneath the banter. It's both hilarious and horrific to watch Lelaina face the challenge of the job market. Her mom (Swoosie Kurtz) suggests that she try Burgerama. When Lelaina points out that she was valedictorian at her university, she's told, "You don't have to put that down on your application." It turns out Lelaina's math isn't good enough to hack it as a fast-food cashier. She fails her interview for a reporting spot at the *Houston Chronicle* when an editor (Anne Meara, half of the comedy team of Stiller and Meara, who are Ben Stiller's parents) asks Lelaina to define irony. "I know it when I see it," says Lelaina, who can't find the words.

Ryder is luminous. She can crack a joke one minute and crush your heart the next without breaking character or letting the acting show. She also brings a prickly intelligence to bear when the role gives her the chance, though Stiller is often content to let the camera stare at her just being adorable. Who can blame him? But the spine Ryder brought to her roles in *Heathers* and *The Age of Innocence* makes us long for stronger stuff. It comes when Ryder digs in to a scene that shows Lelaina hiding from the world under a blanket in front of a blaring TV while chain-smoking and taking advice from a phone-in shrink. Vickie takes one look and cracks: "You are in the bell jar."

What distinguishes the movie is the way it seems to catch characters off guard. Take a simple conversation at a diner. Vickie is worried about her AIDS test, and humor helps her and Lelaina deflect their fears. "I feel like I'm on a crappy show like *Melrose Place*," says Vickie. "I'm the HIV character who it's okay to be nice to, but then I die, and everybody comes to my funeral dressed in chokers and halter tops." Lelaina stifles a laugh before replying, "*Melrose Place* is a really good show." Who says this girl doesn't know irony?

Reality Bites is at its smartest when it stays messiest, when Stiller can't resist squeezing in more good stuff. His fiancée, Jeanne Tripplehorn, appears as a Cindy Crawford fashion clone; Ryder's boyfriend, Dave Pirner, shows up in one of Lelaina's video interviews. The result is like a party that is no less enjoyable for being out of control. You may think *Reality Bites* is just a bunch of white kids sitting around whining. If so, what's your glitch? It's also pure entertainment.   ~ *Peter Travers*

THE HOUSE OF THE SPIRITS

Rolling Stone, *March 10, 1994*

IT'S ALWAYS PAINFUL WHEN A BRILLIANT BOOK becomes a bust of a movie. Consider the fate of the first novel by journalist Isabel Allende – a relative of the Chilean president Salvador Allende, who was killed in a coup in 1973. Allende's saga, stretching from the 1920s to the 1970s, used a tale of sorrow, blood and love in Latin America to strike a universal chord. The 1985 book demanded major talents to bring it to the screen. And it got them. Danish director-writer Bille August (*Pelle the Conqueror*) assembled a cast headed by Britain's Jeremy Irons and Vanessa Redgrave, America's Meryl Streep, Glenn Close and Winona Ryder, Germany's Armin Mueller-Stahl and Spain's Antonio Banderas. It sounds formidable until you realize that this polyglot acting troupe is meant to share national and family ties.

Whoops. Irons is hardly ideal casting as the macho, rapacious patriarch Esteban Trueba. Even in thick pancake make-up (and a thicker accent), he looks better suited for high tea than for pillaging governments and peasant girls. Streep also fights a losing battle. As Trueba's ethereal wife, Clara, possessed of the power to see her family's future, she seems gripped less by spirits than by a galloping dementia. Ryder is Blanca, the daughter of these two unlikely Chileans. By virtue of underplaying, Ryder doesn't embarrass herself, at least not until her prison torture scenes. Blanca rebels by bedding Pedro (Banderas), the revolutionary son of her father's foreman. Banderas's Spanish accent is authentic, which makes him seem oddly out of place in a cast that includes Redgrave and Mueller-Stahl as Clara's parents.

Only Close as Ferula, Trueba's spinster sister, manages to grasp Allende's point about the evolution of feminine consciousness in a world ruled by men. August keeps the rest of Allende's *Spirits* decidedly earthbound. No matter. The movie will vanish quickly; the book will endure. ~ *Peter Travers*

SiSTER ACT

{ BY TRISH DEITCH ROHRER }

US, *December 1994*

Winona Ryder, buttoned into a floor-length bustled dress, sits on an antique couch in a warmly lit Nineteenth-Century living room that is really part of a Vancouver soundstage. She primly licks the white ice cream out of an orange creamsicle. Beside her, sitting straight up in a black Victorian suit, Eric Stoltz sucks on a fudgesicle. They're giggling and licking and looking out at nothing – occasionally at each other from the corners of their eyes – taking a break, side by side, on the set of *Little Women*. Suddenly, Ryder begins to swing her left leg, crossed over her right, while she licks and laughs. From under her skirts and her slips and her hoop swings one foot, in and out, giving us a view of both feet: In the midst of all this Louisa May Alcott-ian Nineteenth Century-ness, Ryder has on black Cons, no socks.

Outside the soundstage, where the sky is a perfect, clean, blue bowl, the film's publicist stands under an eave, looking out over a great grassy square surrounded by various fake facades: a florist, a city hall, a brownstone on Park Avenue. She's pressing a cellular phone to her ear and saying: "O.J. Simpson? I can't *believe* this . . . ," while trying to flag down any young man in shorts and a tool belt or one of the women hustling by, her butt buried in hundred-year-old fabric, her authentic hem dragging behind her. The publicist quietly but frantically shouts the news about O.J., the gun, the freeway and the chase, following it all secondhand as it unfolds.

But trouble back home is far away on this peaceful Canadian day, and it's clear to those who've been on movie sets before that this one is under the spell of many good witches.

Little Women, like the story surrounding its making, is not about women fighting for equality or women proving themselves better than men; it's about how, under even the meanest circumstances, some women bloom into the most magnificent of humans and go on to create environments in which others can bloom.

Winona Ryder has spent years searching for an alternative to the violent thrillers her peers seem drawn to act in. When her friend Denise Di Novi, the coproducer of *Batman Returns,* brought *Little Women* to Ryder's attention, the twenty-three-year-old actress knew she was in. "I have these friends in Petaluma – twelve-year-old girls, actually – and they were so excited about *Little Women.* This is verbatim – they said to me, 'We're aching to see a movie about girls that aren't girlfriends and aren't just cute.'"

Set to open on Christmas Day, *Little Women* is

adapted from Louisa May Alcott's 1868 semiautobiographical novel about four daughters – Jo, Amy, Beth and Meg – who grow through their adolescence materially very poor but spiritually very rich under the love and supervision of their mother, Marmee. Amy Pascal, the Columbia exec in charge of the *Little Women* project (who was named Amy Beth some thirty-odd years ago after two of the characters in the book), has wanted to make this movie for years. In her first job at Warner Bros., she and her friend, script writer Robin Swicord (*The Perez Family),* had intended to adapt the book for the screen, but in the early Eighties, studios weren't making that kind of film – family, period, expensive sets and costumes.

Years later, though, when Pascal moved to Columbia Studios and was suddenly in a position to oversee an adaptation of *Little Women,* she called Swicord, and together they talked about Beth's agoraphobia, Meg's reluctance to eat. Swicord had learned that Alcott's mother was the first paid social worker in Massachusetts, at a home for battered women. Running through both Alcott's life and her novel, Swicord and Pascal decided, were so many threads tying the story to the present and to the concerns of girls growing up today that *Little Women* had the makings of a powerful modern drama in period dress.

Between shots, a woman from costuming stands

behind Susan Sarandon, lifts the back of her dress – her hands lost in layers of white petticoats – and attempts to reposition an infant-size pillow around her sacrum. In front of Sarandon, her youngest son, Miles, a two-year-old blond beauty, frets in his nanny's arms. Sarandon leans toward the boy and begins to wag her butt back and forth, singing, "Pitcher's got a big butt, pitcher's got a big butt." Miles forgets that he's captive and laughs and sings with his mom, who, the next minute, is gone.

"When I saw Susan [Sarandon] marching at a pro-choice rally in Washington with her children," Di Novi says from the stoop of a New York brownstone façade on the set, "I knew she was Marmee."

Asked about this later, Sarandon laughs and says, "I wonder if that was the one where I was pregnant with the third?"

According to Swicord, when Pascal brought the script

to her colleagues at Columbia (most of them men), they green-lighted the project – with certain stipulations: They insisted that Pascal cast a star as Jo and that the budget not exceed $15 million, which is nearly impossible for a period piece with big-name actors.

Later, Swicord says, the filmmakers heard the studio had just given the go-ahead for an action pic with Sean Connery, and the starting budget was more than $50 million. "We all walked around," she says, "hitting ourselves in the head with blunt objects."

Lunch is being served outside in the square from a

catering truck. Sarandon rushes by in her pink-and-white-striped bathrobe, a tall, thin young man with a headset and a clipboard running behind her. Ryder's boyfriend, Dave Pirner of Soul Asylum, stands alone near the salad bar.

Twelve-year-old Kiki – Kirsten Dunst, who plays Amy as a young girl – comes out in full costume and drops a crate and a little table on the lawn. Eva, Sarandon's nine-year-old daughter, sets a punch bowl down, too. The two girls sit together – one with long blond braids and a full-length, drab-green dress, the other a stick-straight brunette in shorts and a T-shirt. Kiki begins to shout, "Lemonade, twenty-five cents!" And the crew nearby – who've spent weeks on this set with children up the wazoo – ignore her. Sarandon comes by, in costume, with Miles in tow, and doesn't stop when Kiki says, "Do you want to buy some lemonade, seeing as you're the mother?" Sarandon says, "I have to get touched up right away," and takes long strides while her son, hand in his mother's, runs to keep up.

The young women playing the four daughters – Ryder, Dunst, Trini Alvarado *(The Babe)* and Claire Danes *(My So-Called Life)* – had already grown close to one another before Sarandon arrived.

"You want everybody to be okay, not to be alone nights or lonely on the weekends," says Gillian Armstrong, the director. "But the girls liked each other from the beginning. Winona rode in the van, even though it was in her contract to have a car and driver."

On the set, after Armstrong has yelled "Cut!" in a loud, shrill voice, a woman comes by with a basket of food. Alvarado comes off the set with a carrot stick. Immediately another woman is there, fussing with Alvarado's hair while yet another lifts Alvarado's hem and begins sewing. But the actress, all dark wavy hair and gray-blue eyes, is like a fighter coming out of the ring: She doesn't acknowledge the people buzzing around her like bees around their queen. She takes small bites of her carrot and talks to Ryder, who's also being fussed over. Someone holds a camera a few feet from Alvarado's face and says, "Flashing, flashing, flashing," as the bulb pops three times, but the girls continue to talk as if they weren't on this set with these people working around them.

The benefits of working in a supportive female environment have proved so enjoyable to Ryder that she is repeating the experience. As

RYDER CONFERS WITH HER DIRECTOR GILLIAN ARMSTRONG ON THE SET OF 'LITTLE WOMEN'

soon as she completes *Boys,* directed by Stacy Cochran *(My New Gun),* she's off to do Jocelyn Moorhouse's *How to Make an American Quilt.* Ryder says of a preproduction meeting for the movie: "There was the woman writer, the woman director and two female executives, and I was hanging out with all these really superpowerful women, and thinking, 'This is how power should be depicted.' It wasn't this ugly, climbing thing. They were respectful."

You don't expect to find ideology on a Hollywood film set along with the peanut M&Ms and the potato chips. There were no arguments around Armstrong's camera while shooting *Little Women,* no catfights or squabbles or anyone defending her ideals; that occurred only when the press started narrowing in, looking for a pigeon-hole. Sarandon was unhappy to hear a journalist refer to *Little Women* as a "feminist film." "When men make a film, it's not called a 'men's film,'" she says. "Why should this be called a 'women's film,' a 'feminist film' – like it's something special – and not a film that filmmakers who happened to be women made? This is important to me."

Swicord see things differently. "I don't agree with Susan. I think when people hear the word *feminism,* they get scared. I think the word has to be used for people to begin to get comfortable with it. But it's important that people express their different opinions."

Armstrong levels it out: "This is a woman's coming-of-age story, and it naturally would be told by the women. It's not *Stand by Me.*"

The picnic tables are now empty, the sunlight a little less bright. In a small trailer, Kiki and Eva wash out their punch bowl and fit their crate into a nook.

The publicist is still standing under an eave talking on the phone to Los Angeles.

On the set, young players hang tinsel and hide presents, the smell of pine in the air. The excitement of Christmas Eve in a house filled with children ripples through the Nineteenth-Century living room and spreads out over the rest of the soundstage. Kiki joins her colleagues in the bright light, and Eva stands beside the camera, looking in. Miles rubs his eyes in his nanny's arms, and Swicord's two daughters each hold one of their mother's hands.

Armstrong yells, "Action!" and the five actresses gather around the piano and begin to sing "Deck the Halls." But they can't get it right. The canned music keeps going, and they get tipped off, fall off, forget the words, sing out of tune. The music person comes to straighten them out, but the four sisters aren't listening: They're wandering off together, singing "Deck the Halls" at their own pace, with their own rhythm, swinging their hips, snapping their fingers, having a good time, being little women. Ⓦ

 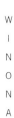

I'VE JUST HAD ONE OF THE
GREATEST TIMES
I'VE EVER HAD MAKING A MOVIE
[MAKING 'LITTLE WOMEN']
BECAUSE I REALLY
TRULY LOVE EVERYBODY
SO MUCH. I KNOW
IT SOUNDS CLICHÉ
BUT THE GIRLS REALLY
DO FEEL LIKE MY
SISTERS, YOU KNOW?

LITTLE WOMEN

US, *January 1995*

Winona Ryder, Susan Sarandon and director Gillian Armstrong are just some of the talents behind *Little Women,* a remake that could well prove as empowering for the training-bra set as the Power Rangers have been to the sandbox contingent. But to call it a women's picture is a misnomer. Men, too, have plenty to learn from these sisters.

Rolling Stone, *January 26, 1995*

WINONA RYDER SPARKS the cast of *Little Women,* a new film version of that 1868 literary sugar rush by Louisa May Alcott. Challenging roles for women are so few these days that this artfully sewn doily – featuring Ryder, Claire Danes, Trini Alvarado, Kirsten Dunst, Samantha Mathis, and Susan Sarandon as the mother of them all – is being hailed as a breakthrough. It's still the same old candy-assed valentine to the March girls of New England. While dear Father goes off to the Civil War, the women soldier on at home. Director Gillian Armstrong (*My Brilliant Career*) and screenwriter Robin Swicord sneak in a few feminist digs at backward males who seek to deny women education, suffrage, sexual freedom and financial independence. But the 1933 film version, directed by George Cukor with a never-better Katherine Hepburn in the Ryder role, did that, too, and without the cloying self-congratulation. One longs to see such a group of power women tackle misogyny with more brimstone and less treacle. But today's smartest actresses are letting themselves get mired in marshmallow. *~Peter Travers*

HOW TO MAKE an american QUILT

Rolling Stone, *November 2, 1995*

WHEN WAS THE LAST TIME you saw a film where hers was as big as his? The size of a role, I mean. Not in *Batman Forever* or *Die Hard With a Vengeance* or *Pulp Fiction* or any of the male-buddy hits that have dominated the Hollywood landscape since Butch met Sundance. Women can't cajole or threaten men to grant them parity in the same movie, so they've decided to take on the boys at their own game. It's war. In this corner, the female-bonding movie, in which women gather to share histories, feelings and the dirt done to them by men. No action – just talk, talk, talk. It's enough to drop a guy in the first round.

How to Make an American Quilt – how's that for a title to scare off the testosterone crowd? – stars Winona Ryder as a Berkeley graduate student who seeks romantic counsel from grandmother Ellen Burstyn, great aunt Anne Bancroft and their quilting-bee friends Maya Angelou, Kate Nelligan, Jean Simmons, Lois Smith and Alfre Woodard. Terrific actresses, yes, and director Jocelyn Moorhouse and screenwriter Jane Anderson pay hat-in-hand tribute to Whitney Otto's best-selling novel. But watching these Joy Quilt Clubbers stitching fabric and reliving their young lives in a flashback is enough to test the tear-jerker tolerance of even the most rabid male feminists. ~ *Peter Travers*

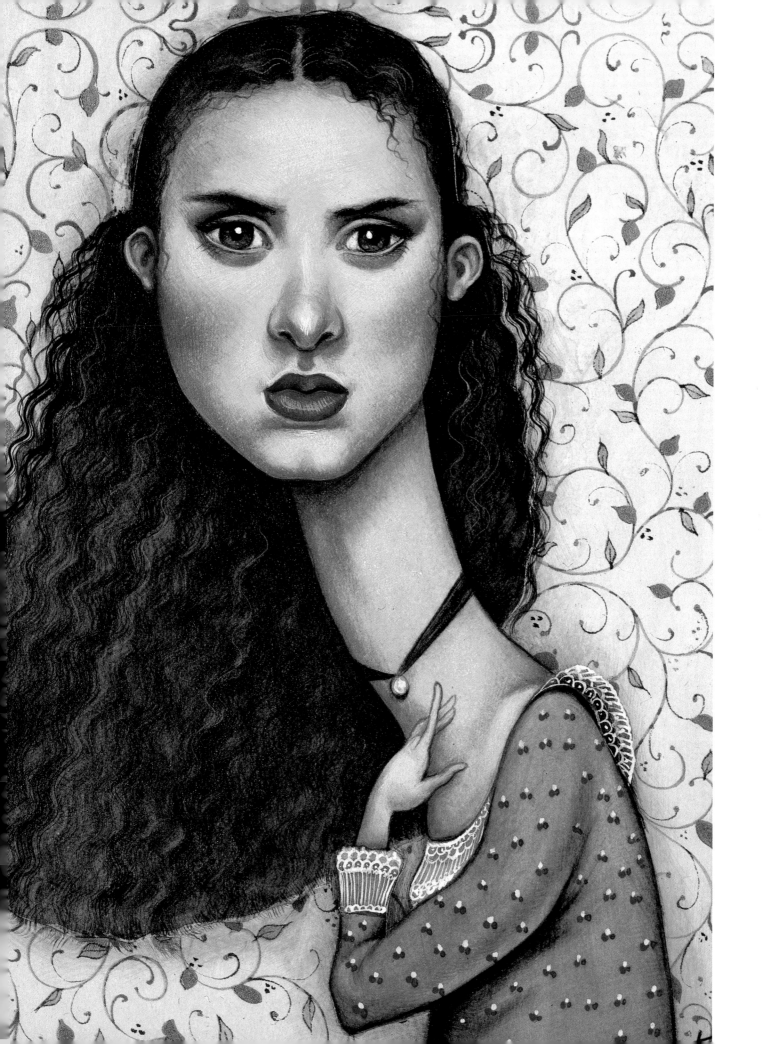

BOYS ARE MORE SUSCEPTIBLE TO SEDUCTION THEY'RE WIMPS WHEN IT COMES TO THAT KIND OF STUFF THEY WANT IT ALL ALL OF A SUDDEN. BOYS DON'T BELIEVE IN GRADUAL ANYTHING. A LOT OF THEM ARE CLUELESS, THE WAY THEY DON'T THINK IT COULD EVER VANISH ONCE THEY HAVE IT ALL THEY THINK THEY'LL STAY HOT FOREVER

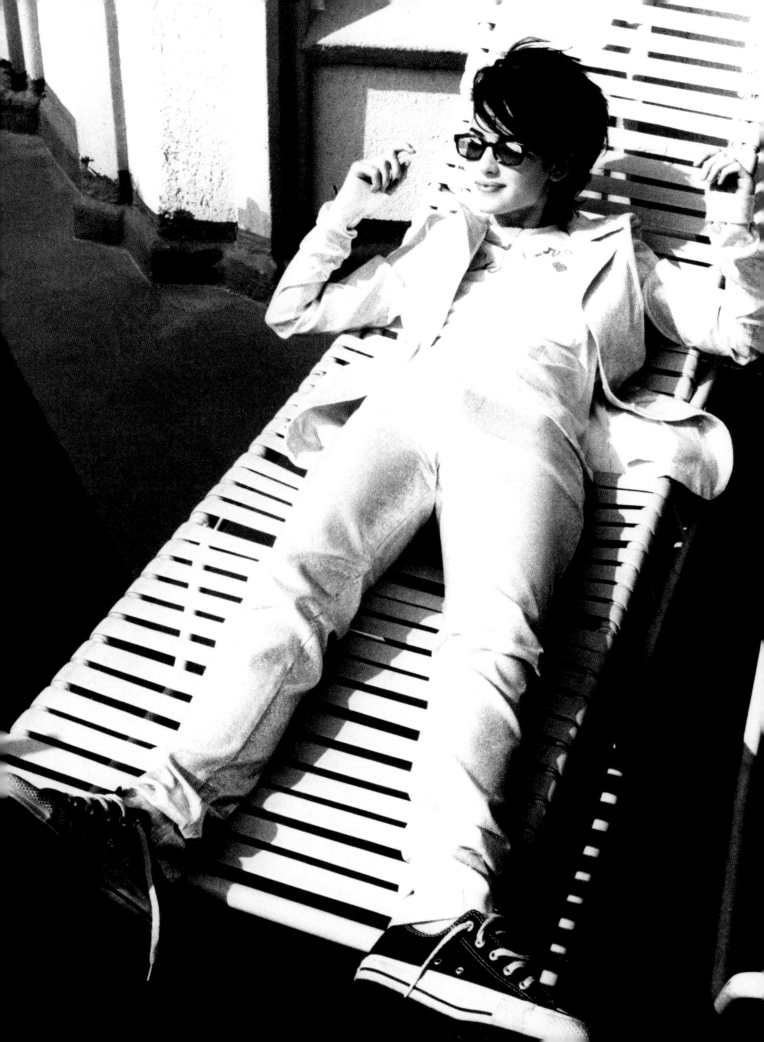

Soul Asylum's DAVE PIRNER

{ By Neil Strauss }

Rolling Stone, *June 29, 1995*

TO SPEND TIME WITH SOUL ASYLUM is to learn how to sleep from nine to five, when the rest of the world is out punching buttons and lifting crates. In fourteen years of music making, Soul Asylum have slowly contorted their lives to adapt to rock & roll's unusual hours of touring and performing. Rock & roll has not always treated the band well; in fact, it almost split the group up several times. But the Minneapolis quartet persevered, and in 1993 its luck changed, almost too dramatically. Unlike Soul Asylum's bad luck, their good fortune can be explained in two words: "Runaway Train," their runaway hit.

Today, Soul Asylum aren't the same band they once were. They're a little self-conscious, a little insecure, a little nervous. After all, it's not easy for a band brought up on a steady diet of punk to accept success without some embarrassment.

With *Let Your Dim Light Shine,* Soul Asylum's first album since the success of "Runaway Train," they must prove that they are bigger, better and, ultimately, more important than "Runaway Train." In other words, they must prove that the

right kind of band can overcome the wrong kind of fame.

Making the challenge even more difficult is the fact that these former Minneapolis punks have pulled what seem to be a few star-trip moves recently:

1. They fired their longtime drummer, Grant Young, and replaced him with an ex-pickup drummer for Duran Duran and David Bowie (Sterling Campbell).

2. Their lead singer and songwriter, Dave Pirner, left his girlfriend of thirteen years to date a movie star (Winona Ryder).

3. The band has not just jammed with but has had nighttime conversations about being stars with one of rock's heavyweights (Bruce Springsteen).

So now you have the handicaps. Take out your scorecard and prepare yourselves, ladies and gentlemen, for the greatest battle of the decade – or at least of the next few pages: Soul Asylum vs. *Rolling Stone.* In three sizzling rounds you will be drawn ever closer to the answer to the most nagging

of musical conundrums: Who can stay up later, a rock band or a rock magazine?

{ROUND ONE}

"PLEASE BUST MY CHOPS, because I'm in the mood to have my chops busted," Dave Pirner says. It's just after midnight, and the straggly looking thirty-one-year-old with a baby face is standing in a hotel lounge in Austin, Texas, announcing his arrival. He's only been in Texas for a half hour, and the battle has already begun. It wouldn't be the first time his chops were busted today, either. At the airport, security reprimanded him after a passenger on his flight from New York complained about Pirner's foul language.

"I've been fucked with just enough where I'm going to start to draw the line," Pirner says in his distinct voice, half space cadet, half dorm-room philosopher. He wipes away a greasy blond dreadlock out of his face and continues: "I'm just going to disappear – really. Faster and faster, the more pressure people put on me. I'm going to, what's the word, *introvert* and go away. And I'm trying to talk myself into that."

For good?

"Yes, for good," says Pirner. "And maybe this has never been done before, but I'd like to beat the system. I would like to have the coup of just having been in a great rock band that nobody cares about anymore. Don't you think I could do that? Here I am for the first time in my life with the fucking greatest band in the world, and I am going to disappear. I will take the band out there on the road and give it to the people with a certain sense of pride. But at one point or another, they're going to have to understand that if they miss the show this year, it might be the last show. You know? It might."

But then again, it might not. Pirner is in a strange mood tonight. Six hours ago he brought more than four months of work to an end by approving final mixes for the songs on Soul Asylum's sixth album, *Let Your Dim Light Shine,* and he hasn't yet recovered from the intensely single-minded process that is the recording of a record. Tonight he wants to see how provocative he can be, how many arguments he can start. He's also fighting an inner battle between his confidence in his songwriting and his insecurity about how the public perceives him.

"My aspiration is to stand alone," Pirner says in an extremely lucid moment, "to put myself on a pedestal and to hate myself for standing on a pedestal."

At the root of Pirner's confusion is success. He's thinking about how Kurt Cobain dealt with it, how Bruce Springsteen deals with it. "I wouldn't kill myself, because that's been done

already," Pirner says. "I think about it sometimes, though."

Springsteen, a sometime late-night confidant of Pirner's, knows the dilemma well. "Dave and I sort of talk on the phone a little," Springsteen says. "It was a pretty confusing experience when I was that age. Being worried about [being a rock star] is good in my opinion. I was always worried about it. I don't know if it helped, but I know that it was good to worry about."

As the hours tick by, the beer empties, various Soul Asylum members come upstairs to bid Pirner good night, and the conversation grows more surreal. Pirner has a few things on his mind – things that may have something remotely to do with music – and seems dead set on unloading them. Picture, if you will, a hotel lounge. Pirner sits on a sofa, engaged in what seems to be a heated conversation with a reporter. Drummer Sterling Campbell sits on a chair to their right, leaning in closely.

Pirner: But look, Socrates was fucking Greek, man. I mean, what influence has that culture had on us people now? Those wrapped-up leaves with rice in them . . .

[*Soul Asylum's publicist arrives.*]

Pirner: I mean, that shit doesn't taste that good, but it tastes pretty good. And you kind of sit there, and you eat it, and go, "All right, these motherfuckers, they ate this shit, and they made a bunch of motherfuckers drag fucking rocks up a hill to build some big old colossal thing. And they tried to create this whole society." And what was the food left over from that? These fucking grape leaves wrapped around rice.

Publicist: I have a recommendation to make as a publicist. You guys could stay up all night talking, but the on-the-record portion of the interview should be over at this point.

Campbell: No, no, no, no.

Pirner: I think I can be held accountable for anything that I should say. I'll tell you what I want to know, though. What's *Rolling Stone*'s angle here? Do they think we're rock stars and suck or what? What do they want to know about us, just between me and you?

Publicist: [*coughs*] What would be the most natural, obvious question to answer that? The new record? Coming off the tremendous success of *Grave Dancers Union*?

Pirner: I mean, what the fuck could possibly be interesting about us?

[*The publicist is silent.*]

Pirner: Exactly. That's the right answer.

Publicist: [*flustered*] Is the tape

recorder running? Could you turn it off?

It's a losing battle for the publicist, and he departs for his hotel. It's past two now, and the beer is gone. Pirner pees in a nearby vase; there is no toilet to be found except for the sink, which is being used by Campbell. Just as he's zipping up, Campbell's girlfriend comes upstairs to drag him off to bed. Most nights with Soul Asylum are like this. First, guitarist Dan Murphy starts yawning and goes to his room to sleep. Then bassist Karl Mueller starts yawning, and he goes to his room to sleep. Then Campbell's girlfriend starts whispering in Campbell's ear, and he goes to bed (not necessarily to sleep). Then Dave Pirner talks, drinks, smokes, plays guitar, hangs out. No one knows if he really goes to sleep or not. It's like a tree falling in the forest: Does it make a sound if no one's around to hear it?

"It doesn't matter to me how late Dave stays up," says Mueller, "as long as we can still do our jobs onstage. If Dan gets up at 8:00 a.m. to look around some town and he's tired by the end of the night, that's no different. The good thing about staying up late is that you have time to yourself to think about things or, in the case of Dave, to write."

It's 6:00 a.m., and Pirner is in his hotel r̶o̶o̶m̶ ̶w̶i̶t̶h̶ new stash of beer – neither thinking nor w̶r̶i̶t̶i̶n̶g̶ ̶a̶n̶d̶ Kraig Johnson, a longtime friend from the M̶i̶n̶n̶e̶a̶p̶o̶l̶i̶s̶ bands Run Westy Run and Golden Smog, th̶e̶ ̶l̶a̶t̶t̶e̶r̶ ̶a̶ country-tinged band featuring Dan Murphy. Pi̶r̶n̶e̶r̶ ̶i̶s̶ ̶g̶azing at the generic lights of the city outside his̶ ̶w̶i̶n̶d̶o̶w. "Where are we?" he asks. It's the third time that P̶i̶r̶n̶e̶r̶ has wondered what city he is in and the first time the question hasn't been answered.

"I don't want to know where I am," Pirner says with a sigh, "because then I'll get upset."

It may seem like Pirner's joking, but the truth is that he has a serious problem with orientation. Even when he gets off the elevator in his hotel, he invariably turns in the direction away from his room. "I have no sense of direction," he says. "I think it's because my mother was so bad with directions. I spent most of my childhood in the back seat of the car watching her get lost." During Pirner's one and only year in college, studying political science at the University of Minnesota, he never made it to his classes on time because he couldn't find the buildings they were in.

"It's real hard to come to terms with the idea that I should be held responsible for finding my way to the grocery store," Pirner says. "There's a certain part of my brain that is just so devoted to music that it becomes a disabler. Remembering phone numbers is more difficult for me than the average person because I'm always trying to remember a melody I thought of earlier. It's a total absent-minded-professor kind of thing. I put the crackers in the refrigerator, and it's just because I'm thinking about other things while I'm having a cracker. And it's frustrating, because it's like 'Why did you put the crackers in the refrigerator, Dave?' And I don't even remember doing it. I never forget a face, though."

There are three bags in Pirner's room. In them, says Pirner, are all the possessions he owns in the world: clothes, notebooks and an acoustic guitar. Of these, what's most important to him are the notebooks in which he writes songs. That's why he has photocopied them all, squeezed them into two shoe boxes and left the duplicates with a friend in Manhattan. He has no tape deck, radio or CD player; he amuses himself by reading comic books or walking around art galleries. Spread out across the room is a colorful array of socks. "Socks are my favorite clothes," Pirner says, pulling up a pant leg to reveal a red-and-black striped one. "These socks cost twenty-five dollars. I love socks, though I always lose them."

Pirner collapses on the bed, spilling beer on the covers in the process, and picks up his guitar. "Shouldn't a got so loaded/ Damn near exploded," he sings, drawling the first line from "To My Own Devices," a song from the new album that almost seems like a plea for help. He hands the guitar to Johnson, who sings some Waylon Jennings, Townes Van Zandt and Woody Guthrie as Pirner plays percussion on a telephone book.

The sun rises, and I wonder if I'm keeping Pirner from sleeping. So I make my excuses.

"We were just getting warmed up," Pirner says as I walk out the door. At the time, I think he's kidding, but the next night, I find out he's not.

Soul Asylum: 1, *Rolling Stone:* 0.

{ROUND TWO}

"I THINK DAVE IS in some kind of battle of the minds with you," Murphy says the next day. But it's not just a battle of the minds or a battle to see who is more credible. It is a battle to see who can stay up the latest. This is made clear just before Soul Asylum's concert at the Terrace, in Austin.

"You shouldn't have gone to sleep last night," Pirner says backstage. "We stayed up and got eggs and screwdrivers from room service when it opened."

In concert, Pirner's exhaustion doesn't show. The band leaves the audience dumbfounded, performing all fourteen songs from *Let Your Dim Light Shine* – even though the album hasn't been released yet – and tossing in only one familiar song, "Somebody to Shove," from 1992's *Grave Dancers Union.* The band does an impressive job working out its new material onstage: Pirner has to apologize only twice for being underrehearsed.

Watching Soul Asylum onstage, it becomes clear that although Pirner gets all the gossip-page ink because he's dating a Hollywood celebrity, Soul Asylum are not a one-man show. Murphy's harmony vocals and clanging guitar add a necessary edge to each song, and Mueller seems to be the only band member able to hold Pirner's lofty lines and Murphy's burning guitar together. If Pirner is air and Murphy's fire, Mueller is solid earth.

"Karl is this band's grounding," says Murphy. "Without him, we would never have been together for so long."

"It's the same thing with any troupe of people," says Mueller in his tired-sounding deadpan. "Somebody's always volatile, somebody's kind of steady, somebody's the most creative or talented. It's whatever comes natural – and for me it's to be steady and keep things even."

After the concert, the band piles into a van and drives to a nearby club where its Minneapolis pals the Jayhawks are playing. Pirner is more than happy with Campbell's perfor-

with music during waking hours, Murphy has a wife, a five-year-old son from a former relationship and a longtime interest in antique trading.

"I can see myself settling in to having the Sanford and Son of all Sanford and Son junk shops," Murphy says. "I just have a life that is so different and far away from the music. Going to auctions is really relaxing for me – like a trip to the shrink. But, you know" – he scratches his chin and reconsiders – "somehow I always find myself pursuing popular-culture shit from the Twenties and Thirties. Maybe that's because I have some unworked-out guilt about being in Soul Asylum, so I'm trying to find popular cultures from other generations."

As different as Murphy is from Pirner, they share one concern: the Grammy-winning "Runaway Train." "I feel like I have to fight for the integrity of this band," says Murphy, "and I think everybody in the band feels that way. We're having this big moral issue now of whether we're going to play 'Runaway Train' on our tour. And I constantly have to stick up for that song and the video and the fact other people are playing it. I think we're really defensive about it. It's a new experience and a new struggle that we have now when interviewers come in saying, 'What's it feel like to be a successful band?' And 'How do you follow up a successful album?'"

mance, his second ever with the band.

"For the first time in fourteen years, I've got the right drummer," Pirner says. "Sterling falls on every consonant and syllable that I've always imagined was the right one."

"Okay, enough, man, I'm in the band now," Campbell says. But the rest of the band is just as hot on Campbell. "Before, Dave's songs were the strongest, but our performances didn't always do them justice," says Murphy, who is being a little too modest, especially since he cowrote one of the best songs on the new album, "Promises Broken."

"Promises Broken" is a gentle, bittersweet song that pivots on the phrase "take me home," which Murphy sings with all the poignancy he can muster. It's a song that aches not just with the pangs of absent love but also the sheer exhaustion of touring.

"There's a line about the Hotel Satellite in the song," Murphy says. "And the Hotel Satellite is pay-per-view. I was sitting in Arizona when we were touring with the Spin Doctors two years ago, and I was flipping through the channels, and all of a sudden I saw this thing about Dave on some news show. That's how I came up with the line 'From the Hotel Satellite/Don't look like you're living right.' It's kind of a dig – but in a friendly way. I have so much respect for Dave musically. But I think he's consumed with music in a way that's really not healthy."

Murphy is a perfect counterweight for Pirner. Where Pirner talks in abstractions, Murphy speaks plainly. Where Pirner frets about his place in rock history, Murphy advocates a strict policy of playing without thinking. Where Pirner is obsessed

IT'S ABOUT TIME Soul Asylum have to answer those questions; after all, it's taken six albums. Soul Asylum were born in the apartment of Murphy's sister, where Murphy and Mueller were living after high school. One night after a particularly inspiring Iggy Pop show, Murphy suggested that Mueller start learning the bass. A week or two later, after another inspiring punk show, the two plugged their instruments into a single guitar amp and performed their first song together: "Bodies," by the Sex Pistols. After that, Mueller approached Pirner, whom Mueller met while working as a carryout boy, about playing drums.

"I didn't have a big revelation that told me that I should be in a rock band or anything," says Mueller, whose realistic outlook probably stems from the fact his parents were librarians. "When I first heard the Clash and the Vibrators, I knew there was something going on. And I'd see the Replacements and Hüsker Dü and say, 'These guys aren't any older than me, and I don't know that they're any smarter, so why shouldn't I do it?'"

The band kicked around Minneapolis's thriving punk scene under the name Loud Fast Rules. They switched Pirner to guitar and vocals because he didn't cut the mustard as a drummer and recorded their first album, 1984's *Say What You Will. . . .*

Back then, the band's art was in the high volume at which it played. The songwriting came later, around 1986, with its second album, *Made to Be Broken.* On it, punk and pop play tug of war with folky ballads on one side, thrashing noise on the other and Pirner's hoarse, edgy voice smack dab in the middle.

In 1987, Soul Asylum signed their first major-label deal, with A&M, and things started going downhill quickly. They made the mistake of trying to record their second A&M album, *And the Horse They Rode In On,* on a soundstage to replicate a live feel and ended up with a weak-sounding record. After the poor promotion and poor sales of *And the Horse They Rode In On,* the band decided to leave the label. But leaving was not an easy task. Soul Asylum had to fork over $200,000 to break their contract and spent the next four years paying the label an equally outrageous amount in back pay.

"It was frustrating," Murphy says. "But you get over being bitter, and you just feel fucking hurt."

It was almost the end of the band: Everyone in it was back at his day job or contemplating returning until Oliver Stone came along.

"I went and saw that terrible Oliver Stone movie about the Doors," says Murphy. "And I remember leaving the theater and just feeling fucking empty. I was like 'That's right. I was

in a band that had a chance to be something.'"

So Soul Asylum reformed and recorded *Grave Dancers Union* for Columbia and put their best foot forward with a well-produced mix that captured the group's ragged glory. From the power pop of "Somebody to Shove" to the trudging country of "Keep It Up" to the punk crashing of "99%" (not to mention "Runaway Train," which rocked an MTV nation), there's not a stinker on the album. Now, as Pirner says sarcastically, everyone expects Soul Asylum to be "the big, crappy voice of a generation."

But with *Let Your Dim Light Shine,* Soul Asylum retain their own voice. There's the catchy power pop ("Misery"), the trudging country ("To My Own Devices") and the punk crashing ("Caged Rat"), plus ultraschlocky late-Seventies hard rock ("Crawl") and, as an album closer, a song that describes a woman's trip to the outhouse ("Just Like Anyone").

"We didn't really worry too much about what people expected when we recorded this album," Murphy says. "But we thought about it a little. I remember Dave called one night. He was all freaked out about whether people would like it. I said, 'Well, you're a fucking songwriter: You write songs, chances are they're pretty good,' because we're very critical of ourselves."

At the Jayhawks show, Benjie Gordon, the A&R person who signed Soul Asylum to Columbia, has an arm drunkenly tossed around one of the big, crappy voices of a generation. Campbell, off to the side, has an imaginary machine gun in his hands, and he's opening fire on Gordon and Pirner and everyone in their vicinity. "There's going to be a race war one of these days, man," Campbell says, continuing to rehearse for

the occasion. He may be joking; he may not be. But we can't worry about it right now because he's not holding a real gun.

Campbell is small and serious and happens to be a genuinely good guy who is capable of turning very intense at times. He has the mind-set of an outsider and feels ostracized from both white society (he feels that some people disapprove of his interracial relationship) and black society (he felt like a misfit growing up listening to Led Zeppelin while his friends were listening to the Ohio Players). He wants to have kids with his girlfriend, but she's only twenty and still living life as if it was here for her benefit. He met her at a club in France. His pickup line: "Smile." (He admits it's a lame line.)

Soul Asylum slowly gather in their van after the concert. Mueller and his wife, Marybeth, arrive first and wait the requisite half hour it takes to gather the rest of the troops. It must suck traveling in groups. "You don't know how much I hate it," Mueller confirms.

Murphy and his wife, Bonnie, decide to find their own way back to the hotel.

He has seen just about enough of the band during the past dozen years. "Karl, Dave and I have been together for so long," he says, "that when we're on a tour bus, we have nothing to say to each other. We can't be like 'Remember the time?' because we've all heard it a million times."

Around 2:30 a.m., a typical evening back at Soul Asylum's hotel begins: Murphy leaves to go to sleep, Mueller leaves to go to sleep, Campbell leaves to go to bed, and Pirner stays up, talking with wide-eyed wonder about tonight's universal enigmas and unsuccessfully trying to pick fights over petty points.

At 5:30, the alcohol is long gone, and Pirner's eyes are hanging heavy. Once the front desk sends up a replacement key for his room (he lost his), he turns in for bed, and those left in the room enjoy the victory of having stayed up later than Pirner.

Soul Asylum: 1, *Rolling Stone:* 1.

{ROUND THREE}

THE SCENE: ANOTHER HOTEL ROOM in another city. On a glass tabletop sit two wine bottles, one of which is empty.

Pirner: Okay. Like, 70 percent of this *Rolling Stone* article is going to be bullshit, man, about what you think this band is about. And you're going to pick out some quotes to support what you think is going to fit your take on the band. And what pisses me off is that I have no fucking idea what your take on this band is. Dude, you're twenty-six.

Me: I should never have told you I was younger than you.

Pirner: I know, you shouldn't have. But let's talk about it. It's exciting to me because I think you're a hotshot. I think you're more happening than I am. And I think you have some sort of angle on me. You're going to pit me against Courtney Love and Mike D. But I've met Yanni. I probably know more about Yanni than you do.

Me: You probably do.

Pirner: I probably do. So me and you are going to try to conduct a good interview, and you're going to write an article telling me something I don't know about the band.

Me: I'm not writing this article for you. I'm writing it for the people who listen to your music.

Pirner: Honestly, what do people fucking care about musicians and the music they make? I don't think they fucking care. And I don't need this article, I don't need this interview. But to tell you the truth, I'd like it if you could make me into someone other than my material. But you've got a project on your hands. And you've got a bunch of pretty dysfunctional guys to talk to.

The conversation gets even more bizarre after this point. But between Round Two and Round Three, someone seems to have taught Pirner how to say, "Off the record." And not only has Pirner made the rest of this part of the debate off the record, he has requested that every time he says the word *totally* that it be stricken from the record. That is probably an abuse of the privilege.

Off the record is an option

Pirner uses when talking about Winona Ryder, who hereafter will be referred to by the pet name that Pirner uses for her when in the company of others: Girlfriend. In the seventeen hours we spend together today, he only mentions her name twice. Once to say that he was upset at being called Ryder's boy toy in these pages a year and a half ago and a second time to explain why he sang her name at a recent show at Tramps, in New York, the show during which Bruce Springsteen popped onstage to duet on "Tracks of My Tears."

"It's tough not to bring your friends into your music sometimes," Pirner says. "So there's this lyric in a song that I kind of changed. It goes, 'I've been to Minnesota/I've been to Arizona/Oh Lord, you know, I've been to Winona.' And I was thinking about the city called Winona. But obviously I was playing off the double-entendre involved. I guess at this point I should either say, 'Next question,' or I should talk about it."

Instead, Pirner avoids the topic altogether by talking about how he would punch out any punk-fanzine editor who would dare to ask him how his credibility is affected by his relationship.

Pirner and his girlfriend met when Soul Asylum taped their *MTV Unplugged* special two years ago. What they have in common is that they are sensitive, thinking people who hate being part of the celebrity system; what sets them apart are Pirner's extreme hours and his nomadic lifestyle. Pirner says they are supposed to move from Los Angeles to San Francisco soon, a decision that not even Soul Asylum's manager has been informed of. But Pirner has a little problem: "I always manage to be somewhere else or out of town whenever I have to move. My friends get mad at me about this."

The problem with moving is not laziness but Pirner's addiction to the road. "With Soul Asylum, I learned to be on the road," he says. "And now, more than my friends, more than my band, I trust the road. If I lost everything, if my girlfriend dumped me and the band got rid of me, you know what I'd do? I'd just travel around like Woody Guthrie, doing solo concerts. And in the middle of a show, I'd ask if anyone had a place to stay, and even if there were forty people there, some fifty-year-old guy or some sixteen-year-old girl would take me in."

Pirner's home is the hotel, any hotel. Propped up against various surfaces in this particular hotel room are black-and-white postcards of such musicians as Billie Holiday and Miles Davis. Pirner takes them wherever he goes, setting them up in each hotel suite so that the rooms all have something in common that is personal to him. The Miles Davis postcard always sits on Pirner's bedside table. This glimmer of a desire for stability is a strange vestige of Pirner's relatively balanced upbringing.

"My parents are kind of high-concept working people," Pirner says. "My dad was a salesman, and my mom was an artist. They set me up to be the most even-keeled, most normal, natural person that anyone could ever be. I'm not saying my parents were less fucked up than anyone else's parents, but they were devoted to their kids. And I am reaping the benefits of that. To think that they had four kids in the family" – he pauses and stares at the ceiling — "Oh, Christ, I'm talking about my family."

Pirner continues after he's convinced that his family is pertinent to who he is as an artist. "My relationship with my family was something totally different ten years ago," he says. "Ten years ago I would have said, 'Dysfunctional family. Worthless, middle-class, boring American family.' We didn't hug, we didn't say we loved one another, we didn't have any of that. Now I look back on my family almost like I'm ready to reestablish my relationship with them. My dad just retired, and I had strong differences with my dad. Now he's got enough time on his hands that he'd want to talk to me. I want to change my dad's ways, I want to talk to him about the stuff we disagreed about when I was eighteen. He means a lot to me, and he didn't mean anything before."

Pirner's love of music started early, thanks to his mother, who insisted that he take up an instrument. "She preferred the piano," he says. "But I wanted to play trumpet because it only had three buttons, and the piano had seventysomething. It was a totally self-defeating proposition, because here I was thinking I was going to master the trumpet because it only had three buttons. But less buttons, the more interpretative physical things you have to do to coax notes out of it."

Pirner joined his middle-school jazz band, where two different trombonists tried to turn him on to rock & roll. One had a Todd Rundgren record, and the other had a Hendrix record. Pirner learned to love rock & roll via the latter.

When it comes down to it, Pirner says, his two biggest influences were not Hendrix and his mother but his high-school English teacher and the legendary bluesman Robert Johnson. "As a lyricist, I owe more probably to my ninth-grade English teacher than I do to anyone," Pirner says, snacking off a tray piled with room service's finest delicacies. "And, of course, she was the meanest, hardest teacher, and everybody thought I was a total square for taking her class. But she was also very passionate about what she taught, and my older sister said, 'If you want to understand the language, Dave, you should check this teacher out.'

"I remember one day somebody asked her what she did on her summer vacation," says Pirner, "and she went into this thing about sitting on a tree swing. She described it in this way that was so passionately literate and made the moment so magical, and she got teary — and she's, like, this sixty-five-year-old woman. It just made me understand why she was so hard on her students, because she was trying to make them understand the power of the English language and poetry. And it appealed to me in a way that I will never forget because nobody had ever illustrated anything to me with that kind of passion."

The effect didn't sink in immediately, however. With his high school band, the Shitz, Pirner wrote his first song ever. "It was 99 percent attitude and 1 percent what the fuck am I doing," he says. "It was called 'Screw, Screw, Screw,' and it was the only song I've ever written about sex. And I got it out of the way from Point One. And now I don't write songs about sex, I don't write love songs, I don't write songs about being on the road because it's all been beaten mercilessly into the ground."

Pirner, believe it or not, was once somewhat of a jock. He played hockey for twelve years as a kid and football in high school. He is probably one of the few popular rock songwriters who can proudly say that he was never a loser in high school. But, he says, "I never thought that I was an appealing individual until I wrote an appealing song."

Pirner leaves his hotel room to take in a concert by the Washington, D.C., hardcore pioneers Fugazi, during which he inches up to the fourth row without being recognized (or at least acknowledged) by Fugazi's high-principled fans. After the show, he closes a local bar and continues talking about how he aspires to have Fugazi singer Ian MacKaye's credibility, Bob Dylan's credibility and Miles Davis's credibility.

"I met Bill Clinton," Pirner says. "And I do think my aspirations are fucking higher than his, man."

Back in the hotel around 7:30 a.m., something very strange happens. Pirner and I have been in his room with no one else present for more than three hours, and the only mind-altering substance he has had (to my knowledge) is alcohol. Suddenly he asks, "Who were we just talking to?"

The answer, of course, is no one. But Pirner persists: "It was somebody that was totally busting my balls for the past three hours. It wasn't even you, man. I remember watching you actually explaining to the other dude how you had to leave. And I was totally uninvolved in the whole thing."

The facts are that I have to go, and maybe Pirner is in denial. He keeps hitting me on the knee when he's talking, as if to jolt me into complete consciousness. I try to escape, but Pirner's not having any of it. He offers every temptation to keep me in the room. First he starts firing off provocative statements about how he's the most important songwriter in the world right now.

"Challenge me!" Pirner says. "I dare you to challenge me on anything! I want to be challenged! I am so fucking credible! Name one way in which I'm not credible."

Housekeeping knocks on the door. Pirner sends the woman away and pulls out all the stops.

"Fire any question at me, man," Pirner insists, rapping my knee. "I can answer any question. Ask me anything you want, and I'll give you the best answer I could ever give you."

I could ask him why he's so insecure about saying his girlfriend's name, how his girlfriend feels about his lifestyle, whether his alcohol intake worries him. But the answers are obvious. So I leave Pirner at 9:30 a.m. so he can enjoy the Pyrrhic victory of being the last one awake, though I really do have one question I'd like to ask him: "Are you afraid to be alone?"

Soul Asylum: 2, *Rolling Stone*: 1.

{THE REFEREE'S DECISION}

THE BATTLE IS OVER, but the referee has not yet announced the victor. In a surprise decision, the following night Soul Asylum's manager, Danny Heaps, announces that what seemed to have been a decisive victory for Soul Asylum in Round Three was actually a tie. "I went to wake Dave at one o'clock today," Heaps says. "It took me an hour. But when he finally opened his eyes, the first thing he said was, 'I think he beat me, man.'"

Soul Asylum: 2, *Rolling Stone*: 2. **W**

{ R E V I E W S }

BOYS

FOR A MOVIE that basically puts a Nineties spin on *Snow White and the Seven Dwarfs,* with Winona Ryder as a runaway babe given shelter by horny teens in a prep-school dorm, *Boys* should be more fun. For a movie adapted from the short story "Twenty Minutes," by the gifted James Salter, *Boys* should be more literate. For a movie written and directed by Stacy Cochran, whose 1992 debut, *My New Gun,* heralded an astute new talent, *Boys* should be more, well, astute. Instead, Cochran's fable flounders in search of a wryly comic tone that remains stubbornly elusive.

Too bad. Cochran begins the tale with a promising air of mystery, as a cop (the invaluable John C. Reilly) calls on Patty Vare (Ryder) at her Maryland home to ask about a car stolen the night before and about the disappearance of Bud Valentine (*Last Dance*'s Skeet Ulrich), a hot pitcher for Pittsburgh. A nervous Patty claims ignorance and hops on her horse for an afternoon ride. When the horse rears and she's knocked unconscious, Patty's found by Baker (Lukas Haas), a senior at the tie-and-jacket Sherwood School for Boys.

Baker is so besotted by this sleeping princess that the younger students tease him about the "boner" in his pants. But soon the dwarfs, er, boys are all doing little favors for Patty. She doesn't want to go home or to a hospital. Baker does it her way, even when she entices him to join her at a local fair for a few beers and a roll in the grass – offenses that could get him expelled. Ryder and Haas (the big-eyed Amish boy from *Witness* is now past puberty) make adorable flirts. But the fuss the film tries to stir about the kid and the older woman doesn't fly since Ryder, at twenty-four, still looks like jailbait no matter how much she smears Patty with lipstick and badass attitude.

More damagingly, the film lacks the dangerous edge of Salter's haunting story. Flashbacks to Patty's night with Bud don't resonate with the terror of a life thrown out of balance. The happy ending is a miscalculation. It's fine for Snow White to go out with a smile and a song; Patty Vare needed to lie down with darkness. ~ *Peter Travers*

W
I
N
O
N
A

RYDER 129

LOOKING FOR RICHARD

Rolling Stone, *October 31, 1996*

BORED BY THE BARD? Tired of sorting out kings, queens and cousins in history plays like *Richard III?* Step up and let Al Pacino restore your faith in English lit. In two hours methinks he'll have you talking in iambic pentameter. Yes, gang, it's Shakespeare for the stupid.

I'm kidding. But the notion of Pacino making his directing debut with a film in which he and a starry cast, including Winona Ryder, Kevin Spacey and Alec Baldwin, perform snippets of *Richard III* interspersed with actors rehearsing and kibitzing, and Pacino quizzing strangers on the street does sound mighty patronizing. Damn, though, if the film doesn't work like a charm. Pacino has been fine-tuning his labor of love (he shot eighty hours of footage) for four years. His look changes from *Scent of a Woman* (clean-shaven) to *Carlito's Way* (bearded), but his ardor and deflating wit burn steadily on high flame. He shares his feelings with other Richards (Kenneth Branagh, Kevin Kline, a wicked Sir John Gielgud) who have boldly knocked the hunchbacked king off his pedestal to find a pulse. Pacino rises so thrillingly to the dare, you want to see more interpretations. Bring on that just-discovered 1912 silent-film version of the play. Pacino makes looking for Richard a great adventure and outrageous fun. ~ *Peter Travers*

THE CRUCIBLE

Rolling Stone, *December 12, 1996*

CONFESS IT! You're really dreading seeing *The Crucible,* fearing a high-minded thesis of numbing good intentions. Arthur Miller's 1953 play about the witch trials in Salem, Massachusetts, circa 1692, is freighted with enough background history to require a catch-up quiz.

True or false:

(1) Miller's play parallels the Red-baiting hysteria of the 1950s, when the House Un-American Activities Committee, run by a rabid Senator Joe McCarthy, equated communism with Satanism. (True.)

(2) Miller was cited for contempt when he refused to betray friends in the Communist Party by naming names or to urge his wife, Marilyn Monroe, to submit to a photo op with the HUAC chief. (True.)

(3) Current parallels to witch hunts include religious fundamentalism, political correctness, accusations of child abuse at day-care centers and the demonizing of race, abortion, AIDS and rock. (True.)

(4) You need to know all these things to understand and appreciate *The Crucible.* (False.)

Miller is the first to admit that the tale must stand on its own. The playwright, now eighty-one, sat near me at a screening of *The Crucible,* unwittingly intimidating all around him. For the Pulitzer Prize–winning author of *Death of a Salesman,* attention must be paid. Miller asked for none of it. He talked with boyish zest of working with director Nicholas Hytner on recrafting *The Crucible* as a $25 million film that would allow startling imagery to resonate with his language and burst the bounds of the stage.

Does it ever. *The Crucible,* despite some damaging cuts to the text, is a seductively exciting film that crackles with visual energy, passionate provocation and incendiary acting. The mood is electric from the first scene, when fifteen sex-starved teenage girls gather in the Salem forest at night to work out their Puritan repression. Tituba (Charlayne Woodard), a slave from Barbados, has organized a conjuring around a boiling kettle. The girls, boiling with lust, shout the names of boys they desire. Some tear off their clothes and dance naked. Not Betty (Rachael Bella), the daughter of Reverend Paris (Bruce Davison), who recoils as her seventeen-year-old cousin Abigail (Winona Ryder) bashes a rooster against the kettle and drinks blood as a charm to kill Elizabeth (Joan Allen), the scolding, sickly wife of farmer John Proctor (Daniel Day-Lewis). Abigail had worked for the couple and their two sons until Elizabeth discovered John's adultery with Abigail and fired her for being a whore.

This "witching" – a child's fatal attraction misread as devil worship – is talked about but never dramatized in Miller's play. Onscreen, Miller's words are made flesh. Guilt over being caught drives the girls into a frenzy of false accusations. The devil made them do it. Abigail conveniently cites Elizabeth Proctor for witchcraft. The others pick up on the trick, naming anyone they ever resented until nineteen are sentenced to hang by Judge Danforth (Paul Scofield), a deputy governor as

{ REVIEWS }

W I N O N A

130 RYDER

avid to make his reputation as McCarthy was.

Miller's screenplay is a model of adventurous film adaptation, showing a master eager to mine his most-performed play for fresh insights instead of embalming it. Hytner, the British theater wiz who made an auspicious 1994 film debut with *The Madness of King George,* directs with a keen eye. Shooting on Hog Island, Massachusetts, a wildlife sanctuary off the coast, allows Hytner to catch raw nature – the hysterical girls rush into the sea, claiming an evil yellow bird is chasing them from court – and spur the actors to interpretive risks.

Ryder finds the lost child in Abigail, who is usually played as a calculating Lolita. Before unleashing her rage, Abigail presses her face to John's and grabs his crotch. Though he rejects her now, John was once the carnal aggressor. "And now you bid me go dead to all you taught me?" says Abigail, for whom sex is just the short route to a soft word. John, for all his late-blooming principles, has corrupted her youth. Ryder offers a transfixing portrait of warped innocence.

The great Scofield is triumphant, avoiding the easy caricature of Danforth as a fanatic. He brings the role something new: wit. We laugh with this judge, which heightens the horror later when he blinds himself to truth in the name of God and his own ambition. The scene in which he ignores Reverend Hale (Rob Campbell), who knows the girls are faking, and bullies the servant Mary Warren (Karron Graves) into delusion and madness chills the blood.

As the unforgiving wife whose "justice would freeze beer," in the words of her husband, Allen is an absolute stunner in an award-caliber performance that is also a surprising source of warmth. By the seashore, where the pregnant Elizabeth has come to say good-bye to her condemned husband, she tells John, "I once counted myself so plain, so poorly made, that no honest love could come to me." Elizabeth's scene of tender reconciliation is the film's moral core. John need only sign a false confession of witchcraft to save himself from the gallows. Of course, he won't. "Because it is my name," he tells Danforth simply. "Because I cannot have another in my life."

In the film's most complex role, Day-Lewis performs with quiet power. Playing nobility can make actors insufferable, but Day-Lewis keeps John Proctor human even when saddled with smudgy makeup and fake brown teeth for his final scene. *The Crucible,* for all its timely denunciation of persecution masked as piety – take that, Christian right! – comes down to individual resistance and how you search your heart to find it. The years haven't softened the rage against self-betrayal in *The Crucible.* This stirring film lets you feel the heat of Miller's argument and the urgent power of his kick. *~ Peter Travers*

{ 'THE CRUCIBLE' WAS ONE OF THOSE MOVIES WHERE YOU COULDN'T WAIT TO GET TO WORK BECAUSE YOU HAD SUCH GREAT THINGS TO SAY }

(1) RYDER'S FIRST FILM, 'LUCAS'; (2) ROB LOWE, RYDER, 'SQUARE DANCE'; (3) MICHAEL KEATON, RYDER, 'BEETLEJUICE'; (4) RYDER, KIEFER SUTHERLAND, '1969' (5) DENNIS QUAID, RYDER, 'GREAT BALLS OF FIRE!'; (6) CHRISTIAN SLATER, RYDER, 'HEATHERS'; (7) 'WELCOME HOME, ROXY CARMICHAEL'; (8) CHER, RYDER, 'MERMAIDS'; (9) JOHNNY DEPP, RYDER, 'EDWARD SCISSORHANDS'; (10) GENA ROWLANDS, RYDER, 'NIGHT ON EARTH'

A WINONA RYDER FILMOGRAPHY

{ By Peter Travers }

CAN WINONA RYDER ACT? Dumb question. She was still an eighth-grader when she made that clear in her 1986 film debut, *Lucas,* finding a tough core of intelligence and wit in the role of a girl geek who loves a boy geek. Ryder has been honing her talent ever since in diverse roles ranging from the dutiful daughter in *Little Women* to the wanton witch in *The Crucible.* The upcoming *Alien: Resurrection,* Ryder's first fling at sci-fi action, is her twentieth film in a career that has already won her a Golden Globe award, two Oscar nominations and raves from critics, including yours truly.

Look, it's not that Ryder is always on target. She can be miscast (as the hardened older woman in *Boys),* misdirected (by Francis Ford Coppola, no less, in *Bram Stoker's Dracula)* and mannered (the bogus Chilean mysticism of *The House of the Spirits* reduced her to striking poses). No matter. Ryder's natural instincts as an actress are strong enough to deflect a few curveballs. Top directors, including Coppola, Martin Scorsese, Tim Burton, Jim Jarmusch and Gillian Armstrong, are eager to work with her. Her costars read like an Oscar Who's Who – Daniel Day-Lewis, Meryl Streep, Jeremy Irons, Susan Sarandon, Anthony Hopkins and Al Pacino. At her best, which is considerable, Ryder can light up a screen with the skill of a sorceress.

"If I didn't know Winona, I'd hate her just on reputation alone," joked Ryder's *Alien: Resurrection* costar Sigourney Weaver. The occasion for the jest was the Show West convention held in March 1997. The National Association of Theater Owners, made up of film exhibitors whose livelihoods depend on actors who fill theaters, had asked Weaver to present an award to Ryder as the Female Star of the Year. Good call. The question is: What took them so long?

So what if Ryder's first five movies cast her in supporting roles. Her star shone through. *Square Dance* (1987), Ryder's second film, is basically earnest, TV-style mush. As Gemma, a Texas farm girl in flannel, suspenders and unflattering

specs, Ryder nonetheless holds her own in the intimidating company of Jane Alexander and Jason Robards. She retains a charming gawkiness that survives the film's frequent slides into melodrama. Gemma's virginal crush on a retarded man, played by Rob Lowe, ends when he tries to cut off his penis with scissors. You heard me. The best scene comes early, when Gemma's grandfather (Robards) instructs her in the do-si-do art of the square dance. "Don't forget it was me that taught you," says grandpop, recognizing something special in Gemma, just as the veteran Robards seems to recognize the potential in the young Ryder.

In her third film, *Beetlejuice* (1988), Ryder plays Lydia, a junior Vampira in black clothes and ratted hair who befriends the ghosts that haunt her parents' New England home. It's a comedy, Tim Burton–style, and Ryder's second-biggest box office to date (after *Bram Stoker's Dracula*). The actress seems liberated by the chance to play a character for laughs. She's especially funny trying to duck the lewd advances of Michael Keaton's title character, a horny corpse who wants Lydia for his child bride. Not happening, babe.

Ryder does have sex onscreen in her fourth film, *1969* (1988), a turgid Vietnam period piece that would not bear mention except for that film first. As Beth, the kid sister of acid-tripping college student Robert Downey Jr., she has to fight to persuade her brother's war-protesting buddy, Scott (Kiefer Sutherland), that she's not too young to take to bed. The "kid" image continues to haunt Ryder. For all we know, she might look like jailbait into her fifties. Some insiders believe Ryder lost the title role in *Sabrina* because Harrison

Ford in a clinch with Ryder would look like child abuse.

Ryder's youthful dewiness made her perfect for *Great Balls of Fire!* (1989) as Myra, the thirteen-year-old bride of hell-raising rocker Jerry Lee Lewis, overplayed by Dennis Quaid. The heartfelt reality of Ryder's performance lifted the film above the sensationalism surrounding it. Ryder was ready for the star spot. In her next movie, she got it.

Heathers (1989) did the trick. Director Michael Lehmann delivers the ultimate black-comic view of high school with a killingly funny script by Daniel Waters that finally gave Ryder dialogue as smart as she was. As Veronica Sawyer, Ryder begins by sucking up to the three Heathers (Shannen Doherty, Kim Walker and Lisanne Falk) – the most popular megabitches at Westerburg High – and ends up helping to kill two of them and fake their deaths as suicides. It's J.D., the charming psychotic played by Christian Slater, who leads Veronica first into bed and then into butchery.

"I'd do this script for one dollar," Ryder told producer Denise Di Novi. She almost didn't do it at all. Her friends, family and agents thought *Heathers* was too dark. And Waters, who wanted Jennifer Connelly, recalls thinking that "Winona wasn't attractive enough." Years later, Ryder would still tease Waters about it ("Jennifer Connelly, you bastard!"). In fact, *Heathers* is the movie in which Ryder seemed to go, overnight, from elfin cute to extraordinarily beautiful.

Ryder turned sixteen during the shooting of *Heathers,* about the same age Judy Garland was when she shot *The Wizard of Oz. Heathers* was no children's fantasy; it was a hard-nosed satire that required its young star to participate in scenes involving rape, mutilation and murder. By law, Ryder had a teacher on the set who strictly limited the time she could spend before the cameras. Waters recalls how "Winona kept hiking down her dress" in her kissing scenes with Slater. For a nude scene on the grass, Ryder had to wear a body suit.

If Ryder was jumpy on the set of *Heathers,* you could never tell it from what you see onscreen. This is the work of an actress in full command of her craft. Veronica is the conscience of the film. Watch the horror on Ryder's face when Veronica realizes that Heather Number One has swallowed

W
I
N
O
N
A

the juice with the lethal drain cleaner that J.D. put in it and not the drink with the phlegm globber. Ryder plays the scene for real, not laughs. "Dear Diary," says Veronica in voice-over, "it's God versus my boyfriend and God's losing."

J.D. knows how to exploit Veronica's weakness. He knows she's angry that Kurt and Ram, the school's two football heroes, are spreading false rumors that they've used their dicks to stage a swordfight in her mouth. J.D. persuades Veronica to lure the jocks into the woods with the promise of sex, make them strip and then shoot them with a stun gun. The gun, of course, contains real bullets put there by J.D., who feels no remorse. "Kurt and Ram had nothing to offer this school but date rapes and AIDS jokes," he argues. Later, Veronica expresses self-disgust by burning her palm with a car cigarette lighter. In one of the coldest scenes in recent cinema, J.D. lights his cigarette with Veronica's burning flesh.

Ryder delivers the satiric humor of *Heathers* with just the right touch of acid. Listen to her cheer up a suicidal friend: "If you were happy every day of your life, you wouldn't be a human being, you'd be a game-show host." More important, she knows to how to make a joke sting. When J.D. raises a finger to give Veronica the bird, she raises a gun and shoots off the offending digit. Who else but Ryder could get away with that? "It's a godsend that we got Winona," says Di Novi. "She's one of those actors that no matter what they do, you hang in there with them." For proof positive, check out Ryder in the penultimate scene from *Heathers*: J.D., wired with explosives, is about to blow himself up in front of the school while Veronica stares him down. "I'm gonna use your pain to light a cigarette," she tells J.D., in retribution for what he did to her in the car. And so she does. *Heathers* ends with a more sentimental scene – a cop-out, actually – but the image that sticks is of Ryder's Veronica standing in the rubble of J.D.'s ashes, triumphantly puffing away. It would take seven years for Ryder to find another role as nervy, fully developed and artfully designed – Abigail in *The Crucible* – but you cannot watch Ryder in *Heathers* without thinking: This actress can do anything.

WHAT RYDER DID NEXT, sadly, was to star in three 1990 releases of varying quality that failed to stretch her talents. *Welcome Home, Roxy Carmichael,* a flat farce about adoption, was the worst. Ryder followed with the much better *Mermaids,* a comedy – set in the 1960s – lifted by Ryder's buoyant portrayal of a fifteen-year-old Jewish girl obsessed with nuns, impure thoughts and a mother, wryly played by Cher, determined to go forth and sin. In Tim Burton's magical *Edward Scissorhands,* Ryder costarred with then-boyfriend Johnny Depp, who played a creature with blades for hands. It was Depp's picture, leaving Ryder little to do as a blond teen queen.

The juicy 1990 role that everyone wanted Ryder to do, especially director Francis Ford Coppola, was Mary Corleone, the daughter of the mafia don, played by Al Pacino, in *The Godfather, Part III.* Exhaustion forced Ryder to drop out of the film. Disastrously, the director replaced Ryder with his own daughter, the inexperienced Sofia Coppola. It's hard to

watch this disappointing second sequel to a masterpiece without thinking how much poignance Ryder could have added to a crucial character who takes a fatal bullet for the father she loves. Mary Corleone is the best role Ryder never played.

Two years later, when Ryder did work with Coppola in *Bram Stoker's Dracula,* she was used as little more than lovely window dressing, a suitable focus for the mad passion of Gary Oldman's toothy count. What a waste. In 1996, she costarred with the godfather himself, Al Pacino. As star and director of *Looking for Richard* – a documentary about making a film of Shakespeare's *Richard III* – Pacino offered Ryder her first crack at the Bard in the role of Lady Anne. She came through superbly. Lady Anne is usually played by a trained older actress, making it hard to believe that the hunchbacked Richard could seduce a woman whose husband he has just murdered. Ryder leads us to understand Lady Anne's youth and confusion. Though Richard is making sport with her ("Was ever a woman in this humour wooed? Was ever a

are we adding our own personalities to the character, or are we creating different personalities? acting is so strange.

woman in this humour won?"), Lady Anne sees only the man who claims he acted out of love ("to live one hour in your sweet bosom"). That's why she believes Richard's rap. Ryder and Pacino make such an effective team that you long to see them act the whole play instead of snippets. *The Godfather, Part III* seems even more a great opportunity missed.

In 1991, after Ryder's bout with exhaustion, she took the role of Corky, a chain-smoking, foul-mouthed L.A. cabbie in Jim Jarmusch's episodic *Night on Earth.* As Corky drives a casting agent (Gena Rowlands) home to Beverly Hills, this mechanic wanna-be shoves a telephone book under her butt to see above the wheel, blows bubblegum and insults other drivers as "nimrods." Corky shows the nerves of a paratrooper, which is just what the casting agent needs for a new movie. "Nah," says Corky, when the agent offers her a chance to be in the flicks. "I wouldn't want to lose this job."

If Ryder was fed up with Hollywood, too, after the unhappy experience of working with the verbally abusive Francis Ford Coppola on *Bram Stoker's Dracula* in 1992, she rallied the next year with *The Age of Innocence,* directed by Martin Scorsese, widely considered to be the greatest living American filmmaker. In adapting Edith Wharton's 1920 novel, Scorsese boldly ventured beyond the mean streets of New York into the formal trappings of high society. Ryder looked perfectly at home in the period costumes. She had a supporting role as May Welland, a girlish beauty in danger of losing her lawyer husband, Newland Archer (Daniel Day-Lewis), to her passionate cousin Countess Ellen Olenska (Michelle Pfeiffer). It was Ryder's consummate performance, however, that won the film its only acting nomination. No wonder. Without dialogue or a single melodramatic gesture, Ryder showed the guile May was able to muster to trap Newland in an unhappy marriage. Watch Ryder carefully in the scene in which Newland tries to break free by telling May of his desire to travel to India and Japan. "As far as that," she says, smiling sweetly, "I'm afraid you can't, dear, not unless you take me with you, and the doctor wouldn't allow that now." May's announcement of her pregnancy slams the door on Newland's future. A gentleman to the end, he can never leave her. The impact is as devastating as Veronica watching J.D. explode in *Heathers*. But this time the destruction is done delicately, almost in a whisper. Ryder lets us see what Wharton called May's "hard, bright blindness," her inability to accept any disturbance in her carefully constructed world. This is acting of the highest order.

A YEAR AFTER 'THE AGE OF INNOCENCE,' Ryder received another Oscar nomination – this time for Best Actress – in Gillian Armstrong's *Little Women* (1994). Ryder played the strong-willed Jo in the third big-screen adaptation of Louisa May Alcott's novel of four dutiful daughters who help their valiant Marmee (Susan Sarandon) fight the good fight at home during the Civil War. It sounds candy-assed, and despite the respectful reviews, it often is. Ryder's forthright performance helps to lower the sappiness factor, except in her scenes with Gabriel Byrne as Jo's older suitor. Alcott saw these two as misfits. Ha! An actress of surpassing loveliness linked with a romantic Irish actor is the stuff of storybook romance, not the early stirrings of feminism.

You can sympathize with Ryder's desire to make *Little Women* with a female director, a female writer and talented young actresses, including Claire Danes, Kirsten Dunst, Trini Alvarado and Samantha Mathis. In the violent Nineties of *Pulp Fiction,* Ryder turned down the chance to star in Quentin Tarantino's script for *True Romance.* Instead, she opted for the sentiment of Jocelyn Moorhouse's *How to Make an American Quilt* (1995) and the chance to work with such veteran actresses as Anne Bancroft, Ellen Burstyn and Jean Simmons. Virtuous, yes, but dull. When would Ryder let it rip?

Ben Stiller's Gen-X comedy *Reality Bites* (1994) allowed Ryder to trade her period costumes for slacker chic as a college grad adrift in the work force. She showed crack comic timing in scenes with Stiller, Ethan Hawke and especially Janeane Garofalo. But where was the serious contemporary drama in which Ryder could make her mark? Stacy Cochran's *Boys* (1996) sure wasn't it. This retelling of *Snow White and the Seven Dwarfs* set in a prep school for boys had Ryder as a mysterious older woman allegedly robbing the craddle with student Lukas Haas, who looked the same age.

For her next full-throttle role, Ryder returned to period, 1692 to be exact, the time of the infamous witch trials in Salem, Massachusetts. The film is *The Crucible* (1996), director Nicholas Hytner's eruptively exciting adaptation of the acclaimed Arthur Miller play that paralleled the McCarthy witch hunts of the 1950s. Ryder plays the seventeen-year-old servant Abigail Williams. It was another teen role, true, but with a difference. Even in the sexually repressed village of Salem, Abigail has grown up fast. The end of her adulterous affair with farmer John Proctor (Daniel Day-Lewis) has led Abigail to bring false charges of witchcraft against John's wife, Elizabeth (Joan Allen). With the wife out of the way, she believes John will return to her.

Ryder's ferocity as Abigail is astounding. Witch or not, you never doubt Abigail's power. If she wants the other girls to say they have seen Elizabeth Proctor walk with Satan, they will say it. Otherwise, she threatens, "I will come to you in the black of some terrible night and will bring with me a pointy reckoning that will shudder you." No one doubts she means it. Abigail has seen Indians smash her parents' heads on the pillow next to hers. She is one tough cookie.

Ryder also finds the vulnerability in her character. John had seduced Abigail when she worked for his family ("You sweated like a stallion when I came near you"). Now as she reaches for his face or his crotch, Abigail is also reaching for the only human touch she's ever known since the death of her parents. Ryder evokes an indelible sense of innocence corrupted. "I wanted you is all," says Abigail as she begs John to run away with her on a ship. "It's not on a ship we'll meet again, Abby," John retorts, "but in hell." Ryder shows us no sentimental tears in Abigail's eyes as she runs to save herself.

The Crucible offers Ryder's most mature performance to date. Yet one of her lines as Abigail stands out. "Why do you call me child?" she asks Day-Lewis's John. Nearly a decade before, she posed much the same question to Kiefer Sutherland's Scott in *1969.* "I'm not a kid," she insisted. What does Ryder have to do to prove that she's grown up and to move on to roles that allow her to play her own age? Develop projects for herself, of course. She has three films lined up – *The Trials of Maria Barbiella; Girl, Interrupted;* and *Roustabout* (definitely not a remake of the 1964 Elvis Presley musical). All three are stories of vital, powerful women.

Alien: Resurrection, directed by Jean-Pierre Jeunet, lets Ryder get unstuck from the past by leaping into the future to join Sigourney Weaver's Ripley on an intergalactic mission. She claims that a poster of Weaver as Ripley decorated her wall at school, sparking a desire to one day play a female action hero. The role suits her. After receiving her award as Female Star of the Year, Ryder recalled seeing her first film, Disney's *Fantasia,* at the age of three: "My parents told me I ran up and hurled myself against the screen, trying to get inside the movie. I guess I'm still trying to do that." Forget trying. Ryder is already inside, refusing to rest on her laurels and hurling herself at new challenges. Bet on it: The best is yet to come. 🔲

The *Wide* World of

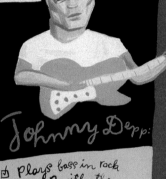

Winona's father was playing a Mitch Ryder record when Winona was choosing a stage name, inspiring the replacement for *Horowitz*

Johnny Depp:

- ☑ Plays bass in rock band P with the Butthole Surfer's Gibby Haynes
- ☑ Part owner of music club Viper Room
- ☑ Her one-time main man

Matthew Sweet wrote a song called Winona - - - -

co-starred with **Cher** in *Mermaids*

There is a Bay-area band called the **Wynona Riders**

Directed a music video for Victoria Williams song "Nature's Way"

Tom Waits

1. on soundtrack during Winona's tax scene in *Night on Earth*
2. Tom Waits appeared in *Bram Stoker's Dracula*
3. *Dracula* co-star Keanu Reeves plays in Dog Star

Dated Soul Asylum lead singer Dave for three years

Dave Pirner & Victoria Williams collaborated on the song "My Ally"

Winona appeared in Soul Asylum video "Without a Trace"

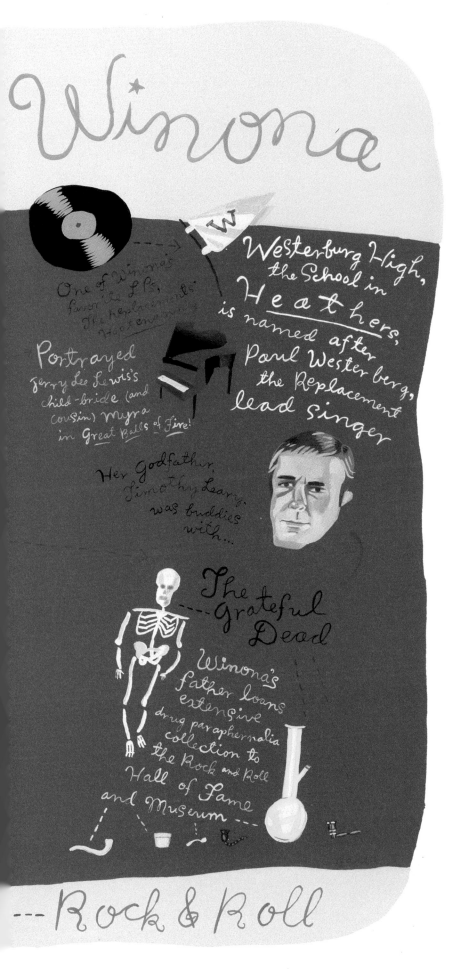

Winona

One of Winona's favorite LPs, the Replacements' Hootenanny

Portrayed Jerry Lee Lewis's child-bride (and cousin) Myra in *Great Balls of Fire!*

Westerburg High, the School in Heathers, is named after Paul Westerberg, the Replacement lead singer

Her Godfather, Timothy Leary, was buddies with...

The Grateful Dead

Winona's father loans extensive drug paraphernalia collection to the Rock and Roll Hall of Fame and Museum

--- Rock & Roll

ROCK & ROLL CONNECTION

WE KNOW SHE loves rock & roll: She quotes Tom Waits lyrics in her journals. She once considered getting the name BUDDY HOLLY tattooed on her ankle. Ex-fiancé Johnny Depp played in bands long before playing in movies; and, of course, Dave Pirner is the consummate rock & roller. What's more: Rock & rollers love Winona. What could be more telling than Utensil, a New York City band formed by a rock publicist and two top rock critics who named themselves after a line Winona utters in *Night on Earth.* Indeed, we hereby crown Winona Ryder the Rock & Roll Queen of Hollywood. **W**

THE MOVIES

LUCAS *(1986)*
Director: David Seltzer
Character: Rina

SQUARE DANCE *(1987)*
Director: Daniel Petrie
Character: Gemma

BEETLEJUICE *(1988)*
Director: Tim Burton
Character: Lydia

1969 *(1988)*
Director: Ernest Thompson
Character: Beth

GREAT BALLS OF FIRE!
(1989)
Director: Jim McBride
Character: Myra Gale Lewis

HEATHERS *(1989)*
Director: Michael Lehmann
Character: Veronica
Sawyer

**WELCOME HOME, ROXY
CARMICHAEL** *(1990)*
Director: Jim Abrahams
Character: Dinky Bosetti

MERMAIDS *(1990)*
Director: Richard Benjamin
Character: Charlotte Flax

EDWARD SCISSORHANDS
(1990)
Director: Tim Burton
Character: Kim Boggs

NIGHT ON EARTH *(1991)*
Director: Jim Jarmusch
Character: Corky

**BRAM STOKER'S
DRACULA** *(1992)*
Director: Francis Ford
Coppola
Character: Mina Harker

THE AGE OF INNOCENCE
(1993)
Director: Martin Scorsese
Character: May Welland

REALITY BITES *(1994)*
Director: Ben Stiller
Character: Lelaina Pierce

**THE HOUSE OF THE
SPIRITS** *(1994)*
Director: Bille August
Character: Blanca Trueba

LITTLE WOMEN *(1994)*
Director: Gillian Armstrong
Character: Jo March

**HOW TO MAKE AN
AMERICAN QUILT** *(1995)*
Director: Jocelyn
Moorhouse
Character: Finn

BOYS *(1996)*
Director: Stacy Cochran
Character: Patty Vare

LOOKING FOR RICHARD
(1996)
Director: Al Pacino
Character: Herself and
Lady Anne

THE CRUCIBLE *(1996)*
Director: Nicholas Hytner
Character: Abigail Williams

ALIEN: RESURRECTION
(1997)
Director: Jean-Pierre Jeunet
Character: Call

Contributors

Chris Chase wrote film reviews for *US* in the late Eighties.

Trish Deitch Rohrer's work has appeared in *US, GQ, Entertainment Weekly, Cosmopolitan, Buzz, Premiere* and *Mirabella.*

David Edelstein has contributed to *Rolling Stone, New York* and *Vanity Fair,* among other publications.

Lawrence Frascella is a New York–based freelance writer who is still writing film reviews. He just completed a novel, *The Family Medium.*

Jeff Giles is a senior writer at *Newsweek* and has written *Rolling Stone* profiles of R.E.M., Robin Williams and many others.

David Handelman was a senior writer at *Rolling Stone* and is currently a contributing editor at *Details.* He hopes someday the world will get to see the lost footage of Winona in a blond wig playing the title character in the Mojo Nixon video "Debbie Gibson Is Pregnant With My Two-Headed Love Child" (a worthier performance than *Boys,* certainly), which Budweiser squashed because of a scene in which a pitbull (a lookalike of its mascot) gets decapitated.

Mark Morrison is the West Coast Editor of *InStyle.*

Barbara O'Dair is the editor of *US.* Formerly the deputy music editor of *Rolling Stone,* she has also worked as a senior editor at *Entertainment Weekly* and the *Village Voice.* She has written for *Rolling Stone, Spin,* the *Village Voice* and other publications. She contributed the introduction to *Madonna: The Rolling Stone Files* and is the editor of *The Rolling Stone Book of Women in Rock: Trouble Girls.*

Steve Pond is a contributing editor at *US* and has been a contributor to *Rolling Stone* since 1979. His work also appears in *Premiere, Movieline* and the *New York Times.*

Neil Strauss is a pop music critic and reporter at the *New York Times* and a regular contributor to *Rolling Stone.* He edited the collection *Radiotext(e)* and has contributed to the Rolling Stone Press books *Cobain* and *Alt-Rock-a-Rama.* He claims to weigh the same as Winona Ryder.

Peter Travers has been *Rolling Stone*'s film critic and senior features editor for film since 1989.

Leslie Van Buskirk is *US* magazine's senior features editor.

David Wild is an *US* and *Rolling Stone* senior writer. He also wrote the introduction to *Crazy Sexy Cool,* by the editors of *US.*

Bill Zehme was a *Rolling Stone* senior writer until 1994 and currently maintains that position at *Esquire.* He is also author of *The Rolling Stone Book of Comedy.*

Photographs

Columbia Pictures Incorporated, All rights reserved, 78 (©1992), 86 (©1993), 111 (©1994), 136 (12) (©1993)

Bill Davila/Retna, 88–89, 124

Patrick Demarchelier, Courtesy of 'Harper's Bazaar,' 144

Everett Collection, 45, 106–107, 134 (2), 135 (1, 4), 136 (13), 137 (14)

A Jim Jarmusch Film, 135 (10)

Brigitte Lacombe, cover, 3, 14, 15, 133, back cover

Annie Leibovitz/ Contact Press Images, 35

Jeffrey Markowitz/ Sygma, 122

Wayne Maser/Visages, 55, 56, 57

Kevin Mazur/London Features, 62

Catherine McGann/ Outline, 72

Terry O'Neill/ Sygma, 41

Sandra-Lee Phipps, 123

Photofest, 134 (3, 5, 6, 8, 9), 135 (7), 136 (15, 18), 137 (11, 16, 17)

Seth Poppel Yearbook Archives, 11

Herb Ritts, 42–43, 65, 68–69, 80–81, 83, 85, 91, 92, 96–97

Matthew Rolston, 76

Albert Sanchez, 71

N. Rica Schiff/Archive Photos, 29

Mark Seliger/ Outline, 119

James Smeal/Ron Galella, 120

Twentieth Century Fox, All rights reserved, 67, (©1990), 137 (19) (©1996)

Max Vadukul/Outline, 7, 9, 13, 20–21

Ellen Von Unwerth/ A+C Anthology, 100, 117, 127, 128–9

Albert Watson, 58

Albert Watson (© Condé Nast P.L.– 'British Vogue'), 99, 109, 113

Theo Westenberger, 30

Firooz Zahedi/Botaish Group, 16

Illustrations

Steve Brodner, 131

Juliette Borda, 140–141

Philip Burke, 38–39

Hungry Dog Studio, 26

Anita Kunz, 115

Robert Risko, 53

Mark Ryden, 105

Janet Woolley, 75

Acknowledgments

Just as the production of a movie requires a team of dedicated souls, so did this book. I'd like to thank those integral to the making of *Winona Ryder:* designer Richard Baker, writer David Wild, film critic Peter Travers, photo editor Fiona McDonagh and *US* editor Barbara O'Dair. As usual, Rolling Stone Press associate editor Shawn Dahl and editorial assistant Ann Abel rose to the task with flying colors. Thanks also to the *US* and *Rolling Stone* writers whose work appears here. The book wouldn't exist if not for Little, Brown's Michael Pietsch and Paul Harrington; ditto, our literary agent Sarah Lazin. Many thanks to *US* and *Rolling Stone*'s Jann S. Wenner, Kent Brownridge, John Lagana, Fred Woodward, Tom Worley and all the many people from the magazines' production department who gave their time (if we ran all their names here this *really* would read like a film's credits), as well as Little, Brown's Teresa Lo Conte, Susan Canavan and Nora Krug. Other invaluable contributors to our project include Joe Ben Plummer, Elsie St. Léger, Susan Richardson, Patricia Romanowski, Will Rigby, Gina Zucker, Tom Soper, Laura Sandlin, Mara Buxbaum, Sha-Mayne Chan, Yoomi Chong, Jennifer Chun, Robert Festino, Amy Goldfarb, Anke Stohlmann, Bess Wong and all the photographers and illustrators whose work graces these pages. And, of course, a big thank you to the talented and intriguing Winona Ryder for inspiring us to create this book.

HOLLY GEORGE-WARREN, editor
ROLLING STONE PRESS
April 1997